Egypt Travel Guide 2023

Unlock the Secrets of the Ancient Land: Your Ultimate Egypt Travel Companion

Garrett Patton

More Books From This Author

Japan Travel Guide 2023

Morocco Travel Guide 2023

New Zealand Travel Guide 2023

Mexico Travel and Adventure Guide

India Travel Guide 2023

Paris Travel and Adventure Guide

Santorini Travel Guide

Florence Travel Guide 2023

Dominican Republic Travel Guide

Sri Lanka Travel Guide

South Africa Travel Guide 2023

EGYPT
TRAVEL GUIDE 2023
GARRETT PATTON

If you have issues with any of the contents of this book or you have questions, I'll be glad to help you.

You can reach me on this email below.

Travelwithgarret62@gmail.com

Table Of Contents

My Experience As A Tourist In Egypt

The sun was just beginning to rise over the horizon, casting a golden glow over the ancient city of Cairo as I stepped out of the airport. I couldn't believe that I was finally here in Egypt, a land steeped in history and mystery.

My first stop was the Great Pyramids of Giza, which loomed in the distance like giant sentinels. As I approached, I could feel the weight of their age and significance, knowing that these structures had been standing for over 4,500 years.

As I walked around the base of the pyramids, I marveled at the incredible engineering that had gone into their construction. How had the ancient Egyptians managed to move these massive stones, some weighing up to 80 tons, into place? The answer, of course, lay in their ingenuity and dedication to their craft.

But the pyramids were just the beginning of my journey through Egypt. Next, I headed to Luxor to explore the Valley of the Kings, the final resting place of the pharaohs of the New Kingdom. As I descended into the tombs, I was struck by the elaborate paintings and hieroglyphs that covered the walls, depicting scenes from the pharaohs' lives and their journey into the afterlife.

But perhaps the most awe-inspiring moment of my trip came when I visited the Temple of Karnak. Walking through the massive columns and halls of the temple, I felt a sense of wonder and reverence for the ancient civilization that had built it. I could almost hear the whispers of the priests and the clang of the bronze bells that once rang throughout the temple.

As my trip came to a close, I couldn't help but feel a sense of sadness at leaving this incredible country. Egypt had captured my heart with its rich history, stunning architecture, and warm, welcoming people. I knew that I would always carry a piece of Egypt with me wherever I went, and that one day, I would return to this magical land once more.

Chapter 1: Introduction To Egypt

History of Egypt

Egypt is a country that is steeped in history, with a rich and fascinating past that has captivated the world for thousands of years. From the pyramids to the pharaohs, the history of Egypt is a story that has captured the imaginations of people from all over the world. In this post, we will explore the history of Egypt, from its earliest beginnings to the present day.

The Beginnings of Egypt

Egypt's history dates back to the Paleolithic period, around 40,000 years ago, when the first evidence of human habitation in the Nile Valley was discovered. The earliest known human settlement in Egypt was at Merimde Beni Salama, in the Delta region of northern Egypt, around 5000 BCE. By 3100 BCE, Egypt was united under the rule of a single king, who is known as Narmer or Menes.

The Old Kingdom

The Old Kingdom period (2686 BCE – 2181 BCE) was a time of great stability and prosperity in Egypt. During this time, the pharaohs of Egypt built the first pyramids, including the Great Pyramid of Giza, which is the largest pyramid in Egypt. The pharaohs of the Old Kingdom also commissioned great works of art and literature, such as the Pyramid Texts and the Coffin Texts, which were used to guide the souls of the deceased through the afterlife.

The Middle Kingdom

The Middle Kingdom period (2055 BCE – 1650 BCE) was a time of change and transition in Egypt. It was during this period that the capital of Egypt was moved to Thebes, in the south of the country. The pharaohs of the Middle Kingdom also began to focus on public works, such as irrigation systems and temples, rather than just the building of pyramids.

The New Kingdom

The New Kingdom period (1550 BCE – 1070 BCE) was a time of great expansion for Egypt. During this time, the pharaohs of Egypt built vast empires, conquering neighboring lands and expanding their influence throughout the region. The New Kingdom pharaohs also built some of the most famous monuments in Egypt, including the temples at Karnak and Luxor, and the Valley of the Kings, where the pharaohs were buried.

The Late Period

The Late Period (664 BCE – 332 BCE) was a time of decline and unrest in Egypt. During this time, Egypt was invaded by foreign powers, including the Persians and the Greeks. The pharaohs of the Late Period were often little more than figureheads, with real power held by foreign rulers and governors.

The Ptolemaic Period

The Ptolemaic period (332 BCE – 30 BCE) was a time of great change in Egypt. After the death of Alexander the Great, Egypt came under the control of the Ptolemaic dynasty, a Greek dynasty that ruled Egypt for nearly 300 years. During this time, Alexandria became the center of Hellenistic culture in the region, and the Library of Alexandria was one of the greatest centers of learning in the ancient world.

The Roman Period

The Roman period (30 BCE – 639 CE) was a time of great change for Egypt. In 30 BCE, Egypt was annexed by the Roman Empire, and became a province of the empire. During this time, the Roman governors of Egypt began to focus on public works, such as the construction of roads and aqueducts, rather than just the building of temples and monuments.

The Islamic Period

The Islamic period (639 CE – present) began with the Arab conquest of Egypt, and the subsequent spread of Islam throughout the region. During this time, Egypt became a center of Islamic learning, and the city of Cairo became one of the most important cities in the Islamic world. The Islamic period in Egypt also saw the construction of many famous monuments, including the Al-Azhar Mosque, the Citadel of Cairo, and the Mosque of Ibn Tulun.

In the 19th and 20th centuries, Egypt underwent a period of modernization and political upheaval. In 1805, Muhammad Ali Pasha, an Albanian soldier, seized power and began a program of modernization and reform, which included the construction of a modern army, the establishment of a centralized government, and the introduction of Western technology and ideas.

In the early 20th century, Egypt became a British protectorate, and remained so until 1952, when a military coup led by Gamal Abdel Nasser overthrew the monarchy and established a republic. Nasser's government focused on modernization and social reform, but also pursued a policy of Arab nationalism and anti-colonialism.

In the years since, Egypt has undergone many changes, including periods of political stability and unrest. The country has faced economic challenges and political turmoil, including the Arab Spring protests of 2011, which led to the ousting of President Hosni Mubarak.

Today, Egypt is a country that is rich in history and culture, with a vibrant economy and a diverse population. The legacy of ancient Egypt can still be seen in the monuments and artifacts that have survived for thousands of years, and the country remains an important center of Islamic culture and learning. The history of

Egypt is a story of endurance, resilience, and cultural richness, and it continues to capture the imagination of people from all over the world.

Geography of Egypt

Egypt is a country located in the northeastern region of Africa, with a small section extending into the southwestern corner of Asia. With an area of approximately 1,002,450 square kilometers, Egypt is the 30th largest country in the world. Egypt is bordered by the Mediterranean Sea to the north, Libya to the west, the Red Sea to the east, and Sudan and Israel to the south.

One of the defining features of Egypt is the Nile River, which flows through the country from south to north, emptying into the Mediterranean Sea. The Nile is the longest river in the world, stretching over 6,650 kilometers. It is also the source of life for Egypt, providing water for irrigation, transportation, and hydroelectric power.

The Nile is also the reason why most of Egypt's population is concentrated along its banks and the adjacent Nile Delta. The Nile Delta is a triangular-shaped area located in the north of Egypt, where the Nile River empties into the Mediterranean Sea. The Delta is one of the most fertile areas in the country, with a rich soil that is ideal for farming. As a result, the Delta is the most densely populated region in Egypt, with over 45 million people living in the area.

Apart from the Nile River and Delta, Egypt is also home to several other important geographic features. The Western Desert, also known as the Libyan Desert, covers about two-thirds of the country's land area. This desert is characterized by its vast sand dunes, rocky plateaus, and deep valleys. The Western Desert is sparsely populated, with most of its inhabitants living in small oases that are scattered throughout the region.

The Eastern Desert, also known as the Arabian Desert, is located to the east of the Nile River and covers about one-third of Egypt's land area. This desert is rich in minerals, including gold and iron, and is home to several important mining operations. The Eastern Desert is also home to the Red Sea Mountains, which run parallel to the Red Sea coast and provide a scenic backdrop for the area.

The Sinai Peninsula is located in the northeastern part of Egypt and is separated from the rest of the country by the Suez Canal. The Sinai Peninsula is bordered by the Mediterranean Sea to the north and the Red Sea to the south and is characterized by its rugged mountain ranges and beautiful coastal areas. The peninsula is a popular tourist destination, with visitors coming to enjoy its beaches, coral reefs, and historic sites.

The geography of Egypt is incredibly diverse, with a range of different landscapes and environments. From the fertile Nile Delta to the vast deserts of the west, Egypt offers a unique blend of natural beauty and cultural heritage. The Nile River remains the lifeblood of the country, providing water and sustenance to millions of people, while the deserts and mountains offer a stark and stunning contrast to the fertile green of the river valley. For anyone interested in exploring the wonders of Africa, Egypt is a must-visit destination.

Why Visit Egypt?

Egypt is one of the most fascinating countries in the world, with a rich and ancient history that continues to captivate visitors from around the globe. From the Pyramids of Giza to the Nile River, Egypt is a place that should be on every traveler's bucket list.

Here are some of the reasons why Egypt is a place to visit:

Ancient History

Egypt is home to some of the most famous ancient sites in the world, including the Pyramids of Giza, the Sphinx, and the Valley of the Kings. These sites offer visitors a glimpse into the history and culture of one of the world's oldest civilizations. The Pyramids of Giza, for example, are over 4,500 years old and were built as tombs for pharaohs.

The Nile River

The Nile River is the lifeblood of Egypt and has played a crucial role in the country's history and development. A Nile River cruise is a great way to see some of Egypt's most famous sites, including the Temple of Karnak and the Temple of Luxor. Visitors can also enjoy the beautiful scenery along the river and witness daily life in rural Egypt.

Beaches

Egypt has some of the most beautiful beaches in the world, including those in Sharm el-Sheikh, Hurghada, and Marsa Alam. These beaches offer crystal-clear waters, stunning coral reefs, and a range of water sports, making them a popular destination for tourists.

Cuisine

Egyptian cuisine is a delicious blend of Mediterranean and Middle Eastern flavors. Dishes like koshari (a mix of rice, lentils, and pasta), ful medames (a hearty fava bean stew), and mahshi (stuffed vegetables) are just a few of the must-try dishes when visiting Egypt.

Culture

Egyptian culture is rich and diverse, with influences from ancient Egypt, Islam, and the Mediterranean. Visitors can experience this culture firsthand by visiting traditional markets, attending cultural events, and exploring local neighborhoods.

Affordable Travel

Egypt is a budget-friendly destination, with affordable accommodations, food, and transportation. This makes it an ideal destination for travelers who want to experience a different culture without breaking the bank.

Friendly People

Egyptians are known for their hospitality and friendliness towards visitors. From the moment you arrive, you'll be welcomed with open arms and treated like family.

Egypt is a place that offers something for everyone, from ancient history to beautiful beaches to delicious cuisine. With its affordability, friendly people, and rich culture, Egypt is a destination that should be on every traveler's list.

Chapter 2: Planning Your Trip To Egypt

Best Time To Visit

When planning a trip to Egypt, one of the most important considerations is timing. The weather, the crowds, and the availability of attractions can all vary depending on the time of year. So, what is the best time to visit Egypt? Let's explore.

The climate in Egypt can be divided into two seasons: a hot and dry summer, and a mild winter. The summer months, from May to September, are scorching and often reach temperatures of over 40°C (104°F). This heat can be unbearable for some, and outdoor activities such as sightseeing and hiking can become uncomfortable. However, the summer months are also the low season for tourism, which means that prices can be lower, and crowds thinner.

On the other hand, the winter months, from October to April, are much cooler and more pleasant, with temperatures ranging from 15-25°C (59-77°F). This is considered the peak tourist season, with many visitors coming to Egypt to escape the cold weather in their home countries. The cooler temperatures make it much easier to explore the outdoor attractions, such as the pyramids and temples, without feeling too uncomfortable.

Another factor to consider when deciding on the best time to visit Egypt is the availability of attractions. Some of the most popular tourist destinations in Egypt, such as the Pyramids of Giza, are open year-round. However, other attractions, such as the temples of Abu Simbel, have more limited availability. The Abu Simbel temples are open all year round, but the best time to visit them is during the winter months when the sun is lower in the sky, creating a stunning visual effect on the temple façade.

In addition to the climate and availability of attractions, it is also important to consider cultural events and festivals. Egypt is a predominantly Muslim country, and Ramadan is a significant event that occurs annually. During Ramadan, many businesses close during the day, and restaurants may only open after sunset. It is important to be respectful of local customs and traditions during this time, but it can also be an incredible opportunity to experience a unique aspect of Egyptian culture.

The best time to visit Egypt depends on individual preferences and priorities. If you can tolerate the heat, the summer months offer lower prices and thinner crowds. However, if you prefer milder temperatures and want to explore all the attractions, the winter months are the peak tourist season. Remember to check the availability of specific attractions and consider cultural events such as Ramadan when planning your trip. Whatever time of year you choose to visit Egypt, you are sure to have an unforgettable experience.

Budgeting and Costs

For travelers planning a trip to Egypt, it is important to consider budgeting and costs to ensure a successful and enjoyable journey. In this post, we will provide you with a detailed and compelling guide on budgeting and costs when traveling to Egypt.

Flight Costs

The first expense to consider when traveling to Egypt is the cost of flights. The cost of flights varies depending on your location, the time of year, and the airline you choose. Generally, flights to Egypt from North America or Europe can range from $500 to $1500. However, you can save some money by booking flights early or during low seasons.

Accommodation Costs

The cost of accommodation in Egypt depends on your preferences and budget. If you're looking to stay in luxury hotels or resorts, you should expect to pay around $150 to $300 per night. For budget-friendly options, you can find hostels or guesthouses that cost around $10 to $30 per night. It's always a good idea to research and compare different accommodation options before booking to find the best deal for you.

Transportation Costs

Transportation is another important factor to consider when budgeting for a trip to Egypt. Taxis and ride-hailing services are available in cities, and prices can vary from $5 to $20 depending on the distance. For longer distances, consider taking a train or bus, which can be much cheaper, with prices ranging from $5 to $30.

Food and Drink Costs

Egypt is known for its delicious and affordable food. Local street food can cost as little as $1, while a meal at a mid-range restaurant can cost around $10 to $20. If you're looking to save money, consider cooking your meals or buying groceries from local markets.

Tour Costs

One of the main reasons people visit Egypt is to explore its ancient landmarks and attractions. Many tour companies offer packages that include transportation, accommodation, and sightseeing activities. Prices for these tours can vary widely, with budget-friendly tours starting at around $50, and luxury tours costing upwards of $1000.

Other Costs

It's important to budget for unexpected expenses such as visas, travel insurance, and souvenirs. Visa fees can range from $15 to $85 depending on your country of origin, while travel insurance can cost anywhere from $50 to $200 depending on the length of your stay and coverage. Souvenirs are a great way to remember your trip, but be sure to budget accordingly.

Budgeting for a trip to Egypt can vary widely depending on your preferences and itinerary. However, it is possible to visit Egypt on a budget without sacrificing quality or experience. By carefully planning and budgeting for your trip, you can ensure a memorable and enjoyable journey to one of the world's most fascinating countries.

Visa and Entry Requirements

Egypt is a country steeped in ancient history, cultural traditions, and natural beauty, making it a popular destination for travelers from around the world. However, before booking a trip to Egypt, it is essential to understand the visa and entry requirements to ensure a smooth and hassle-free journey.

Visa Requirements for Egypt

Egypt has different visa requirements depending on your nationality and the purpose of your visit. Visitors can obtain a visa on arrival or apply for an e-Visa before arrival.

Visa on Arrival

Tourists from eligible countries can obtain a visa on arrival at any international airport in Egypt. The visa is valid for a maximum stay of 30 days and costs around $25. Visitors must have a valid passport with at least six months' validity remaining and a return or onward ticket.

E-Visa

Travelers can also apply for an e-Visa online before arriving in Egypt. The e-Visa is valid for a maximum stay of 30 days and costs around $25. To apply for an e-Visa, visitors must have a valid passport with at least six months' validity remaining and a digital passport photo.

Countries Eligible for Visa on Arrival or e-Visa

Citizens of over 46 countries are eligible for an e-Visa or visa on arrival. Some of these countries include the United States, Canada, United Kingdom, Australia, New Zealand, European Union countries, and many others.

However, it is essential to check the latest visa requirements before traveling, as the list of eligible countries can change frequently.

Entry Requirements for Egypt

Aside from the visa requirements, visitors to Egypt must also meet certain entry requirements.

Passport

All visitors must have a valid passport with at least six months' validity remaining. The passport must also have at least one blank page for the entry stamp.

Proof of Accommodation

Visitors must have proof of accommodation in Egypt, such as a hotel reservation or a letter of invitation from a resident in Egypt.

Proof of Funds

Visitors must also have proof of sufficient funds to cover their stay in Egypt. This can be in the form of cash, credit cards, or a bank statement.

Vaccinations

There are no mandatory vaccinations required for entry into Egypt. However, it is recommended to have vaccinations for hepatitis A, typhoid, and polio. Travelers should also consult with their doctor before traveling to Egypt.

COVID-19 Travel Restrictions

Due to the COVID-19 pandemic, there may be additional travel restrictions and requirements for visitors to Egypt. Visitors must check the latest travel guidelines and restrictions before traveling.

Egypt is a fascinating and culturally rich country that offers a unique travel experience. Visitors must be aware of the visa and entry requirements before traveling to ensure a hassle-free journey. Remember to check the latest guidelines before booking your trip to Egypt to avoid any complications.

What To Pack

Traveling to Egypt can be an incredibly rewarding experience. It's a country steeped in history and culture, with ancient wonders like the pyramids and the Sphinx, as well as modern marvels like the bustling city of Cairo. However, packing for a trip to Egypt can be a bit of a challenge, especially if it's your first time.

Here are some tips on what to pack when traveling to Egypt:

Clothing

Egypt is a conservative country, so it's important to dress modestly. For women, this means covering your shoulders and knees, and avoiding tight-fitting clothing. Loose-fitting, lightweight clothing made of breathable fabric like cotton is ideal, especially during the hot summer months. Long-sleeved shirts and pants are also a good idea to protect your skin from the sun.

Footwear

Comfortable and sturdy shoes are a must when traveling to Egypt. You'll be doing a lot of walking, especially if you're visiting sites like the pyramids or the Valley of the Kings. Sneakers or hiking shoes with good traction are recommended, especially if you're planning to do any hiking or exploring in the desert.

Sun protection

Egypt is known for its hot and sunny weather, so it's important to pack sun protection. This includes a broad-brimmed hat to protect your face and neck from the sun, as well as sunglasses to protect your eyes. Sunscreen with a high SPF is also a must, especially if you have fair skin.

Personal hygiene items

Pack all of your personal hygiene items, including toothpaste, toothbrush, shampoo, soap, and deodorant. These items may be difficult to find or expensive in Egypt, so it's best to bring your own.

Medication

If you take any prescription medications, be sure to bring enough for your entire trip. It's also a good idea to bring over-the-counter medications like pain relievers and antihistamines, as well as any prescription medications for motion sickness, diarrhea, or other common travel ailments.

Electronics

Egypt has a different electrical system than many other countries, so you'll need to bring an adapter for your electronic devices. A power strip with multiple outlets is also useful if you have multiple devices to charge.

Money and Documents

Be sure to bring all necessary travel documents, including your passport, visa, and any vaccination records. It's also a good idea to bring a copy of these documents, in case they get lost or stolen. Bring enough cash or traveler's checks to cover your expenses, as credit cards may not be accepted everywhere.

Insect Repellent

Egypt is home to a variety of insects, including mosquitoes and sand flies, which can carry diseases like malaria and dengue fever. Be sure to bring insect repellent with you and apply it regularly, especially if you're spending time outdoors.

Packing for a trip to Egypt requires a little extra thought and planning, but with the right items in your suitcase, you'll be prepared for a wonderful adventure. Remember to pack modest, lightweight clothing, comfortable shoes, sun protection, personal hygiene items, medications, electronics, travel documents, insect repellent, and enough cash to cover your expenses. With these items in tow, you'll be ready to explore all that Egypt has to offer.

Health and Safety Tips

Egypt is a fascinating destination for travelers from all over the world. From the Pyramids of Giza to the Nile River, the country is full of incredible sights and sounds that will leave you in awe. However, as with any destination, it is important to be aware of potential health and safety risks that may arise during your trip. In this post, we will provide you with some essential health and safety tips to help you enjoy a safe and memorable trip to Egypt.

Vaccinations and Medications

Before traveling to Egypt, it is important to make sure that you have all the necessary vaccinations and medications. The Center for Disease Control and Prevention (CDC) recommends getting vaccinated for Hepatitis A, Hepatitis B, Typhoid, and Rabies. In addition, if you plan on traveling to rural areas, you may need to get vaccinated for Yellow Fever. It is also recommended that you bring some basic medications with you, such as painkillers, antidiarrheals, and motion sickness medication.

Water and Food Safety

One of the most common health risks when traveling to Egypt is food and waterborne illnesses. It is important to only drink bottled water and to make sure that the seal is unbroken before consuming. It is also recommended that you avoid tap water, ice, and any food that has been washed in tap water. In addition, be cautious about consuming street food and raw or undercooked food.

Sun Safety

Egypt is known for its hot and sunny weather, and it is important to protect yourself from the sun. Wear sunscreen with a high SPF, a hat, and sunglasses to protect your skin and eyes from harmful UV rays. Also, try to avoid direct sunlight during the hottest parts of the day and seek shade whenever possible.

Transportation Safety

If you plan on using public transportation, such as taxis or buses, be cautious and only use reputable services. It is also recommended that you avoid traveling alone at night and in remote areas. If you plan on driving, make sure to follow the traffic laws and be aware of the risks associated with driving in Egypt.

Cultural Sensitivity

Egypt is a Muslim country with a conservative culture, and it is important to be respectful of the local customs and traditions. Dress modestly, especially when visiting religious sites, and avoid public displays of affection. It is also recommended that you ask for permission before taking photos of people or places.

Security Precautions

Egypt has experienced political instability and occasional acts of terrorism in the past. It is important to stay informed about the current situation and to avoid any demonstrations or large gatherings. In addition, keep your valuables close to you and avoid carrying large amounts of cash.

Egypt is a beautiful country with a rich history and culture. By taking the necessary health and safety precautions, you can ensure that your trip is both safe and enjoyable. Make sure to research your destination before your trip, and don't hesitate to reach out to local authorities or travel experts if you have any concerns. With a little bit of planning and preparation, you can have a safe and unforgettable trip to Egypt.

Currency and Money Matters

If you're planning a trip to Egypt, it's essential to be aware of currency and money matters to avoid any unnecessary complications during your stay. Egypt's economy heavily relies on tourism, and the country's official currency is the Egyptian Pound (EGP). In this post, we'll discuss everything you need to know about currency and money matters before traveling to Egypt.

Currency Exchange

It's always a good idea to exchange some currency before you arrive in Egypt, but it's not necessary to have all your cash on hand when you arrive. You can exchange your currency at the airport, banks, and authorized exchange offices throughout Egypt. It's essential to be cautious when exchanging money, and you should only use authorized exchange offices to avoid being ripped off.

Egypt has a cash-based economy, and credit cards are not widely accepted, especially outside of the major cities. You may be able to use your credit card in some hotels, restaurants, and shops, but it's always wise to have cash on hand. ATMs are widely available in major cities, and they accept international cards, but be sure to check your bank's international withdrawal fees before you use them.

Cost of Living

The cost of living in Egypt is relatively low compared to other countries, and it's an affordable destination for travelers. However, the cost of living can vary depending on where you're staying and the activities you're doing. In major cities like Cairo and Alexandria, you can expect to pay higher prices for accommodation, food, and transportation than in smaller towns and villages.

When it comes to food and drink, local street food is very affordable, and it's a great way to experience the local cuisine. However, if you prefer to dine in restaurants or cafes, you should expect to pay higher prices. In general, the cost of living in Egypt is very reasonable, and you can enjoy a comfortable trip without breaking the bank.

Tipping Culture

Tipping is a common practice in Egypt, and it's an essential part of the country's culture. It's customary to tip service workers, such as hotel staff, tour guides, drivers, and restaurant servers. The amount of the tip can vary depending on the service provided, but it's typically around 10% of the total bill.

In some cases, a service charge may be included in the bill, but it's still customary to leave an additional tip for good service. You should always carry small bills with you to tip service workers, and it's wise to have some extra cash on hand in case you receive exceptional service.

Currency Restrictions

Egypt has restrictions on the amount of currency that can be brought into the country and taken out of the country. According to Egyptian law, travelers are only allowed to bring up to $10,000 USD or the equivalent in foreign currency into the country without declaring it. If you're carrying more than this amount, you must declare it at customs.

When leaving Egypt, you're allowed to take up to $5,000 USD or the equivalent in foreign currency out of the country without declaring it. If you're carrying more than this amount, you must declare it at customs. It's essential to follow these currency restrictions to avoid any legal complications during your trip.

Currency and money matters are an essential part of planning your trip to Egypt. You should exchange some currency before you arrive, carry small bills for tipping, and be aware of the country's currency restrictions. By following these tips, you can enjoy a comfortable and hassle-free trip to Egypt. Remember to always be cautious when exchanging money and use authorized exchange offices to avoid being ripped off.

Chapter 3: Cultural Experiences

Egyptian Cuisine

Egyptian cuisine is a blend of traditional and modern cooking techniques, ingredients, and flavors that have been influenced by the country's geography, history, and culture. With a rich culinary heritage dating back to the time of the pharaohs, Egyptian cuisine offers a tantalizing array of dishes that are sure to delight foodies and curious travelers alike. In this post, we'll explore some of the most popular Egyptian dishes, their ingredients, and where to find them.

Ful Medames

Ful medames is a traditional breakfast dish made from fava beans that have been slow-cooked and mashed with garlic, lemon juice, and olive oil. The dish is often served with bread and is a staple of the Egyptian diet.

Koshari

Koshari is an Egyptian comfort food that is a mixture of lentils, rice, macaroni, and chickpeas topped with a spicy tomato sauce and fried onions. It's a popular street food and can be found in almost any Egyptian city.

Molokhia

Molokhia is a green leafy vegetable that is a staple in Egyptian cuisine. The leaves are chopped and cooked with garlic and coriander, and then served over rice or bread. It's a hearty and flavorful dish that is perfect for vegetarians and meat lovers alike.

Ta'meya

Ta'meya, also known as falafel, is a popular snack food made from ground fava beans, herbs, and spices that are formed into balls or patties and deep-fried until crispy. It's often served with tahini sauce or stuffed into a pita bread with fresh veggies.

Shawarma

Shawarma is a Middle Eastern dish that has become a popular street food in Egypt. Thinly sliced marinated meat, usually beef or chicken, is grilled on a vertical rotisserie and then wrapped in pita bread with vegetables, pickles, and sauces.

Fattah

Fattah is a classic Egyptian dish that is traditionally served during special occasions like weddings and religious festivals. It's made from layers of bread, rice, and meat, usually lamb or beef, that are topped with a tomato-based sauce and garnished with nuts and herbs.

Umm Ali

Umm Ali is a sweet dessert that is similar to bread pudding. It's made with layers of phyllo pastry, milk, and nuts, and then baked until golden brown. It's often served warm with a dollop of whipped cream or ice cream.

Now that we've mentioned some of the most popular Egyptian dishes, let's talk about where to find them.

Abu Tarek in Cairo

Abu Tarek is a popular restaurant in Cairo that specializes in koshari. It's been serving up the dish for over 75 years and has become a must-visit spot for locals and tourists alike.

Felfela in Cairo

Felfela is a well-known restaurant in Cairo that serves traditional Egyptian food like ful medames, ta'meya, and molokhia. It's a popular spot for lunch and dinner, and the outdoor seating area offers a great view of the city.

El-Fishawy in Cairo

El-Fishawy is a historic café in Cairo's Khan el-Khalili market that has been serving shawarma and other Egyptian street food for over 200 years. It's a great spot to grab a quick bite while exploring the market.

Naguib Mahfouz Café in Cairo

Named after the famous Egyptian author, Naguib Mahfouz Café is a charming café located in the heart of Cairo's Islamic district. The café serves a variety of Egyptian dishes, including fattah, and also offers a cozy atmosphere for those looking to relax and enjoy a meal.

El Abd in Alexandria

El Abd is a seafood restaurant located in Alexandria that has been around since the 1950s. It's known for its delicious grilled fish, including mullet and sea bass, and offers a stunning view of the Mediterranean Sea.

Kebdet El Prince in Alexandria

Kebdet El Prince is a restaurant in Alexandria that specializes in kebabs and liver dishes. It's a popular spot for locals and offers a cozy atmosphere for those looking for a hearty meal.

Al Azhar in Luxor

Al Azhar is a restaurant in Luxor that serves traditional Egyptian cuisine, including koshari, ta'meya, and molokhia. It's located near the Luxor Temple and offers a great view of the Nile River.

There are numerous street vendors and food carts that sell great and genuine Egyptian food in addition to these eateries. These sellers are widespread throughout Egypt's cities and offer a cost-effective method to sample a range of foods.

Egyptian food offers a wide variety of tastes and recipes that are certain to please any food enthusiast. There is something for everyone to enjoy, from ful medames and koshari to shawarma and fattah. There are several eateries and street sellers that serve delectable and genuine Egyptian food, whether you're in Cairo, Alexandria, or Luxor. Try some of these foods the next time you're in Egypt to learn more about its rich culinary tradition.

Festivals and Events

Egypt is a country that is steeped in history and culture, and it is no surprise that it is home to some of the most fascinating and diverse festivals and events in the world. Whether it is celebrating the country's ancient history, its vibrant arts scene, or its modern cultural landscape, there is always something happening in Egypt that is sure to captivate and delight locals and visitors alike.

One of the most popular festivals in Egypt is the Cairo International Film Festival, which takes place annually in November. This event is a showcase of some of the best films from around the world, and it attracts filmmakers, actors, and movie enthusiasts from all over the globe. In addition to film screenings, the festival also features workshops, seminars, and discussions about the art and business of filmmaking.

Another festival that celebrates the arts is the Luxor International Painting Symposium, which takes place in the city of Luxor each year. This event brings together artists from Egypt and around the world to create new works of art inspired by the history and beauty of Luxor. The resulting paintings are then displayed in a public exhibition, and visitors can purchase them to take home as a unique souvenir of their time in Egypt.

Egypt is also home to a number of religious festivals that are steeped in tradition and history. One of the most famous is the Moulid of Sayyid

Ahmed al-Badawi, which takes place in the city of Tanta. This festival celebrates the birth of Sayyid Ahmed al-Badawi, a famous Muslim saint who lived in the 13th century, and it is attended by millions of people each year. Visitors can expect to see colorful parades, hear religious music, and participate in spiritual ceremonies.

For those who are interested in ancient history, there are a number of festivals that celebrate Egypt's rich past. One of the most popular is the Abu Simbel Sun Festival, which takes place twice a year in the city of Abu Simbel. This festival celebrates the alignment of the sun with the temple of Ramses II, which occurs on February 22nd and October 22nd each year. Visitors can witness this incredible event and learn more about the history and significance of the temple.

Another festival that celebrates Egypt's ancient history is the Opet Festival, which takes place in the city of Luxor. This event was first celebrated in ancient times, and it is a celebration of the god Amun, who was believed to be the king of the gods. During the festival, a procession of priests and dignitaries would carry statues of Amun, his wife Mut, and their son Khonsu from the Karnak Temple to the Luxor Temple. Today, the festival has been revived, and visitors can witness this ancient ritual and learn more about the history and beliefs of the ancient Egyptians.

Finally, for those who want to experience modern Egypt, there are a number of festivals that celebrate the country's vibrant culture and contemporary arts scene. One of the most popular is the Cairo Jazz Festival, which brings together jazz musicians from around the world for a week-long celebration of this unique art form. Visitors can enjoy concerts, workshops, and jam sessions, as well as explore the vibrant jazz scene in Cairo.

Another festival that celebrates modern Egyptian culture is the Downtown Contemporary Arts Festival, which takes place in the heart of Cairo each year. This event showcases a wide range of contemporary art forms, including dance, theater, music, and visual art. Visitors can see performances by some of Egypt's most talented artists and explore the dynamic arts scene in this bustling city.

Egypt is a country that offers a diverse and fascinating array of festivals and events, from ancient religious rituals to modern celebrations of the arts. Whether you are interested in history, culture, or contemporary arts, there is always something happening in Egypt that is sure to capture your imagination and leave you with lasting memories.

Now, let's take a closer look at some of the top festivals and events in Egypt that you won't want to miss.

Cairo International Film Festival: As mentioned earlier, this annual event is a must-attend for film enthusiasts. The festival has been running since 1976 and has grown to become one of the most prestigious film festivals in the Middle East and North Africa. The festival showcases films from all over the world, and it attracts some of the biggest names in the film industry. In addition to film screenings, visitors can also attend workshops, seminars, and masterclasses on various aspects of filmmaking.

Abu Simbel Sun Festival: This unique festival is a celebration of the alignment of the sun with the temple of Ramses II in Abu Simbel. Visitors can witness this incredible event twice a year, on February 22nd and October 22nd, as the sun illuminates the temple's inner sanctum, which is normally shrouded in darkness. The festival also includes a colorful parade and a sound and light show that tells the story of the temple's construction and history.

Luxor International Painting Symposium: This event brings together artists from around the world to create new works of art inspired by the history and beauty of Luxor. The resulting paintings are then displayed in a public exhibition, and visitors can purchase them to take home as a unique souvenir of their time in Egypt. The symposium also includes workshops, seminars, and cultural events that allow visitors to experience the rich artistic heritage of Egypt.

Downtown Contemporary Arts Festival: This festival showcases the best of contemporary art in Egypt, including dance, theater, music, and visual art. The festival is held in the heart of Cairo and attracts some of the most talented artists in the country. Visitors can attend performances, exhibitions, and workshops, as well as explore the vibrant arts scene in this bustling city.

Moulid of Sayyid Ahmed al-Badawi: This religious festival celebrates the birth of Sayyid Ahmed al-Badawi, a famous Muslim saint who lived in the 13th century. The festival is held in the city of Tanta and is attended by millions of people each year. Visitors can expect to see colorful parades, hear religious music, and participate in spiritual ceremonies that offer a unique insight into Egypt's rich religious traditions.

These are just a few of the many festivals and events that take place in Egypt throughout the year. From ancient religious rituals to modern celebrations of the arts, there is something for everyone in this fascinating country. So, whether you are a history buff, an art lover, or simply looking for a unique cultural experience, Egypt's festivals and events are sure to leave you with lasting memories.

Shopping in Egypt

Shopping in Egypt is a unique and exhilarating experience that combines modernity and tradition. The country is home to bustling bazaars, high-end shopping malls, and artisanal shops that offer a diverse range of products, from ancient antiques to contemporary fashion. The Egyptian shopping scene is a reflection of the country's rich history, vibrant culture, and eclectic influences.

One of the most popular shopping destinations in Egypt is the Khan El Khalili bazaar. Located in the heart of Old Cairo, this souk is a labyrinth of narrow alleys, crowded stalls, and aromatic cafes. It dates back to the 14th century and is known for its vibrant atmosphere and traditional crafts. Visitors can find everything from handcrafted textiles and pottery to jewelry and spices. Bargaining is a must in Khan El Khalili, and shoppers can test their haggling skills to get the best prices.

For a more upscale shopping experience, head to the Cairo Festival City Mall. This modern mall is home to over 300 stores, including international brands such as Zara, H&M, and Nike. It also features a cinema complex, a food court, and a range of entertainment options. The mall is a great place to escape the hustle and bustle of the city and indulge in some retail therapy.

If you're looking for traditional souvenirs, the Al-Azhar Park craft center is a great place to start. Located in one of Cairo's largest parks, the center features a range of artisanal shops selling handmade crafts such as glassware, ceramics, and textiles. Visitors can also take part in workshops and learn about traditional Egyptian crafts.

When it comes to gem shopping, Egypt has a rich history of producing precious stones such as lapis lazuli, turquoise, and carnelian. The country is also home to some of the world's most famous gemstones, such as the Cleopatra Emerald and the Star of the East diamond.

One of the best places to shop for gems in Egypt is the Khan El Khalili bazaar. Here, visitors can find a range of gemstones, including semi-precious stones such as amethyst, citrine, and peridot, as well as rare gems such as emeralds, rubies, and sapphires. Many of the gemstones are sourced from mines in Egypt, making them a truly authentic souvenir.

Another great place to shop for gems is the Naguib Mahfouz Cafe and Gift Shop. Located in the heart of Khan El Khalili, this shop is known for its beautiful gemstone jewelry, including necklaces, bracelets, and earrings. The shop also offers a range of other souvenirs, such as traditional textiles and pottery.

For those who want to invest in high-end gemstones, the Egypt Gems Company is a great place to start. This company specializes in rare and exotic gems such as alexandrite, tsavorite, and tanzanite. The company has a showroom in Cairo and offers a range of custom designs and bespoke services.

Shopping in Egypt is an experience not to be missed. Whether you're looking for traditional souvenirs or high-end gems, the country has something to offer every shopper. From the bustling bazaars of Khan El Khalili to the modern malls of Cairo, Egypt's shopping scene is a unique blend of history and modernity that will leave you with unforgettable memories.

Egyptian Arts and Craft

Egyptian art and crafts are some of the oldest and most enduring artistic traditions in human history. Dating back over 5,000 years, the art and crafts of ancient Egypt have fascinated people around the world with their exquisite beauty, incredible detail, and rich symbolism. From the grand monuments of the pharaohs to the everyday objects of ancient Egyptian life, these works of art provide a window into one of the world's greatest civilizations.

The art of ancient Egypt was deeply rooted in religion, mythology, and the beliefs of the people. It was also closely tied to the power and prestige of the pharaohs, who commissioned many of the grandest and most impressive works of art. Egyptian art was created to serve many different purposes, from religious and ceremonial to practical and everyday. The artists who created these works of art were highly skilled and trained in the techniques and traditions of their craft, passing down their knowledge from generation to generation.

One of the most recognizable and iconic forms of Egyptian art is the sculpture of the pharaohs. These massive stone statues, often depicting the rulers of Egypt with their arms crossed over their chest, were created to impress and intimidate their subjects. The pharaohs were seen as living gods, and their images were meant to convey their power and authority to the people. Many of these statues were placed in temples and other religious sites, where they could be worshipped and venerated by the people.

Another important form of Egyptian art is the wall paintings and reliefs found in tombs and temples. These works of art often depicted scenes from daily life, as well as myths and legends from Egyptian mythology. The colors used in these paintings were often bright and vibrant, and they were designed to last for eternity. Some of the most famous examples of Egyptian wall paintings can be found in the tombs of the pharaohs in the Valley of the Kings.

Egyptian crafts were just as important as the art, and they played a vital role in the daily life of ancient Egyptians. These crafts included pottery, jewelry making, weaving, and woodworking. The ancient Egyptians were skilled in these crafts and used them to create everyday objects as well as luxury items for the wealthy. Egyptian pottery, for example, was used for storage and transportation of food and other goods, while jewelry was often worn as a symbol of status and wealth.

One of the most impressive examples of Egyptian crafts is the process of mummification. This process was used to preserve the bodies of the pharaohs and other important people after death, so that their spirits could live on in the afterlife. The process involved removing the internal organs, drying the body with natron (a type of salt), and wrapping it in linen bandages. The mummies were then placed in elaborate tombs, filled with treasures and other items they might need in the afterlife.

Egyptian art and crafts are a testament to the skill and creativity of one of the world's greatest civilizations. These works of art have inspired and fascinated people for thousands of years, and they continue to capture the imaginations of people today. Whether it's the grandeur of the pharaohs' monuments or the intricate detail of everyday objects, the art and crafts of ancient Egypt offer a glimpse into a rich and fascinating culture that still has much to teach us today.

Religious Sites

From the ancient worship of the gods and goddesses to the introduction of Christianity and the later arrival of Islam, Egypt has been home to a variety of religious practices and beliefs. As a result, the country boasts a wealth of religious sites that attract visitors from all over the world.

One of the most famous religious sites in Egypt is the Great Sphinx of Giza, which is believed to have been built during the reign of Pharaoh Khafre in the 26th century BCE. The Sphinx is a massive limestone statue of a mythical creature with the head of a human and the body of a lion, and it has long been associated with the ancient Egyptian religion. Many believe that the Sphinx was built to protect the nearby pyramids and temples, and it has since become a symbol of Egypt's ancient history and religious heritage.

Another famous religious site in Egypt is the Temple of Karnak, which was built over a period of almost 2,000 years and was dedicated to the god Amun. The temple complex includes several large temples and many smaller shrines, and it was once one of the most important religious sites in ancient Egypt. The massive columns, intricate carvings, and beautiful statues that adorn the temple are a testament to the skill and artistry of the ancient Egyptian craftsmen.

In addition to these ancient religious sites, Egypt is also home to a number of important Islamic and Christian landmarks. The Al-Azhar Mosque in Cairo is one of the oldest and most famous Islamic universities in the world, and it is a center for Islamic learning and scholarship. The mosque was founded in 970 CE, and it has since become a symbol of Islamic culture and education.

Christianity also has a rich history in Egypt, and there are several important Christian sites throughout the country. The Coptic Orthodox Church of Alexandria is one of the oldest Christian churches in the world, and it is the spiritual center of the Coptic Orthodox community. The church was founded in the first century AD by Saint Mark, one of the apostles of Jesus Christ, and it has played a significant role in the development of Christian theology and tradition.

Another important Christian site in Egypt is the Monastery of Saint Catherine, which is located at the foot of Mount Sinai. The monastery was built in the 6th century AD and is one of the oldest Christian monasteries in the world. It is also believed to be the site where Moses received the Ten Commandments from God, and it has since become a pilgrimage site for Christians and Jews alike.

All things considered, Egypt's holy sites provide an enthralling window into the nation's extensive and varied history and culture. This unique nation has something to offer everyone, whether they are interested in Islamic culture, Christian history, or ancient Egyptian religion.

Chapter 4: Transportation and Accomodation in Egypt

Transportation Options

From the ancient pyramids to the bustling cities, there's no shortage of places to explore. But with so much ground to cover, transportation is key for tourists visiting Egypt. Fortunately, there are several transportation options available, each with its own unique advantages and disadvantages.

Taxis

Taxis are a common sight on the streets of Egypt, particularly in major cities like Cairo and Alexandria. They are readily available and can be hailed from the street or arranged through a hotel or tour operator. Taxis are typically inexpensive, making them a popular choice for budget-conscious travelers.

However, tourists should be aware that taxi drivers in Egypt may not always use meters, so it's important to negotiate the fare upfront. It's also wise to agree on a price before getting into the taxi to avoid any misunderstandings. Additionally, some taxi drivers may try to take advantage of tourists by taking longer routes or insisting on extra fees, so it's important to be vigilant and assertive.

Buses

Buses are another affordable transportation option in Egypt, particularly for those traveling longer distances. There are several bus companies operating throughout the country, with regular routes connecting major cities and tourist destinations.

While buses can be a cost-effective way to get around, they can also be quite crowded and uncomfortable, particularly during peak travel times. Additionally, buses in Egypt may not always run on time, so it's important to factor in extra time when planning your travels.

Trains

Egypt's railway system is one of the oldest in Africa, with trains connecting major cities and tourist destinations throughout the country. Trains are generally a more comfortable and spacious option than buses, with a range of classes available to suit different budgets.

However, tourists should be aware that Egypt's trains can be quite slow, particularly on older lines. Additionally, trains may not always run on time, so it's important to build extra time into your itinerary. It's also wise to book train tickets in advance, particularly during peak travel times when trains can be busy.

Rental cars

For those looking for greater flexibility and independence, rental cars are also available in Egypt. However, tourists should be aware that driving in Egypt can be chaotic and unpredictable, particularly in cities like Cairo. Additionally, road signs may be in Arabic only, making navigation challenging for non-Arabic speakers.

If you do choose to rent a car, it's important to be vigilant on the roads and to have comprehensive insurance coverage. It's also wise to plan your route in advance and to have a GPS or map on hand.

Nile Cruises

For a unique and unforgettable transportation experience, tourists can also opt for a Nile cruise. These cruises typically take several days, with stops at various ancient temples and tourist attractions along the way. Nile cruises offer a comfortable and luxurious way to see some of Egypt's most famous sights, with onboard amenities including swimming pools, restaurants, and entertainment.

However, Nile cruises can be quite expensive, particularly for those on a budget. Additionally, some cruises may not be as environmentally friendly as others, with the potential to harm the delicate ecosystem of the Nile river.

There are several transportation options available for tourists visiting Egypt, each with its own unique advantages and disadvantages. Whether you choose to travel by taxi, bus, train, rental car, or Nile cruise, it's important to do your research and plan your itinerary in advance. With careful planning and a sense of adventure, tourists can experience all the wonders that Egypt has to offer.

Driving in Egypt

Driving in Egypt can be a thrilling and adventurous experience for tourists, but it can also be a bit daunting and overwhelming at first. The roads are often congested, the traffic can be chaotic, and the driving habits of locals may seem unpredictable. However, with a bit of preparation and awareness, tourists can navigate Egypt's roads safely and confidently. Here, we will provide everything you should know about driving in Egypt.

License and Documents

Before renting a car, tourists should make sure they have a valid driving license from their home country or an international driving permit. Additionally, they will need to carry the following documents while driving:

Passport
Visa (if applicable)
Car rental agreement
Car insurance documents
It's essential to keep these documents on hand at all times while driving, as police checkpoints are common, and tourists may be asked to produce them.

Rules of the Road

In Egypt, driving is done on the right side of the road, and the rules of the road follow international standards. However, the driving culture in Egypt is unique, and some local drivers may not follow traffic laws strictly. Here are some of the essential traffic rules tourists should keep in mind:

Speed Limits: The maximum speed limit on highways is 120 km/h (75 mph), but in cities, it varies from 50 to 80 km/h (31 to 50 mph).

Seatbelts: It is mandatory for drivers and front-seat passengers to wear seatbelts. Fines will be imposed for not following this rule.

Traffic Lights: Traffic lights are widespread in cities, but not always followed. Tourists should exercise caution while crossing intersections.

Roundabouts: Roundabouts are common in Egypt, and drivers should give way to vehicles already in the roundabout.

Horns: Horns are used frequently in Egypt, and locals use them to signal their presence on the road. Tourists should use their horns sparingly and only when necessary.

Here are some essential driving tips to follow to ensure a safe and enjoyable driving experience in Egypt:

Plan Your Route: Before embarking on a journey, tourists should plan their route using a GPS or a map. This will help them avoid getting lost or stuck in traffic.

Avoid Rush Hour: Traffic can be heavy during rush hour (7 am-10 am and 4 pm-7 pm), and it's best to avoid driving during these times.

Be Alert: Tourists should be extra vigilant while driving, particularly at night. It's not uncommon to see pedestrians or animals on the road, and it's essential to keep an eye out for them.

Be Patient: Patience is key while driving in Egypt. Traffic can be slow, and drivers may not always follow the rules of the road. Tourists should remain calm and patient, allowing plenty of time to reach their destination.

Avoid Driving Outside Cities: It's best to avoid driving outside cities, particularly in the desert regions. The roads can be poorly maintained, and it's easy to get lost.
Renting a Car:

Tourists can rent a car from international rental agencies or local companies. However, it's essential to choose a reputable rental company and read the terms and conditions carefully before signing the rental agreement. Tourists should also inspect the car thoroughly before taking possession of it and report any damage to the rental company. It's advisable to take out comprehensive insurance, including collision damage waiver (CDW), to cover any damage to the car.

Driving in Egypt can be a bit intimidating for tourists, but with the right preparation, awareness, and patience, it can also be a fun and rewarding experience. Following the traffic rules, being alert, and driving defensively are crucial to ensuring a safe journey. By planning your route, avoiding rush hour, being patient, and renting a car from a reputable company, tourists can have a hassle-free driving experience in Egypt. Here are a few additional things to keep in mind:

Road Conditions

Egypt has a mix of well-maintained highways and poorly-maintained rural roads. In the cities, the roads can be narrow and congested. Tourists should be cautious while driving on rural roads, as they may be unpaved, bumpy, and full of potholes. Additionally, it's not uncommon to see stray animals or pedestrians on the roads.

Parking

Finding parking in the cities can be challenging, and tourists should plan ahead for parking options. Street parking is available in most areas, but it can be hard to find a spot. Paid parking lots and garages are also available in some cities.

Fuel

Petrol stations are plentiful in Egypt, and petrol is relatively inexpensive compared to other countries. Tourists should make sure to fill up their car's tank before embarking on a long journey, as petrol stations may be sparse in rural areas.

Emergency Services

In case of an emergency, tourists should dial 122 for the police, 123 for the ambulance, and 180 for fire services. It's also a good idea to have the contact details of the rental company and car insurance provider on hand.

Driving in Egypt can be an adventure, and it's an excellent way to explore the country's beautiful landscapes and historic sites. However, it's important to follow traffic rules, be alert, and exercise patience while driving. With the right preparation and mindset, tourists can enjoy a safe and rewarding driving experience in Egypt.

Accomodations

Affordable Hotels in Egypt

Egypt is a country rich in history and culture. Its four major cities, Cairo, Alexandria, Luxor, and Aswan, offer visitors a glimpse into the country's ancient past, as well as its modern present. Whether you're a history buff, a foodie, or just looking for a relaxing vacation, there is something for everyone in Egypt.

One of the most important aspects of planning a trip to Egypt is finding affordable accommodations. Fortunately, there are many budget-friendly hotels throughout the country that offer comfortable rooms, great amenities, and easy access to popular tourist attractions. Here are some affordable hotels to consider for your trip to Egypt.

Cairo - Wake Up! Cairo Hostel

Price: $12-$18/night

Located in the heart of Cairo's bustling downtown area, Wake Up! Cairo Hostel is a great choice for budget-conscious travelers. The hostel features both private rooms and dorms, as well as a rooftop terrace with stunning views of the city. Wake Up! Cairo Hostel is within walking distance of many popular tourist attractions, including the Egyptian Museum and Tahrir Square.

Cairo - Lotus Hotel

Price: $18-$30/night

The Lotus Hotel is a budget-friendly option in Cairo's trendy Zamalek neighborhood. The hotel features comfortable rooms with private bathrooms, as well as a rooftop terrace with views of the Nile River. The Lotus Hotel is conveniently located near many of Cairo's top attractions, including the Cairo Tower and the Cairo Opera House.

Cairo - Cecilia Hostel

Price: $14-$20/night

Cecilia Hostel is a great option for budget-conscious travelers looking to stay in the heart of Cairo's historic district. The hostel features both private rooms and dorms, as well as a rooftop terrace with views of the city. Cecilia Hostel is within walking distance of many popular tourist attractions, including the Khan el-Khalili bazaar and the Al-Azhar Mosque.

Alexandria - Alexander The Great Hotel

Price: $30-$45/night

The Alexander The Great Hotel is a budget-friendly option in the heart of Alexandria. The hotel features comfortable rooms with private bathrooms, as well as a rooftop terrace with views of the Mediterranean Sea. The Alexander The Great Hotel is within walking distance of many popular tourist attractions, including the Bibliotheca Alexandrina and the Montazah Palace Gardens.

Alexandria - Paradise Inn Windsor Palace Hotel

Price: $45-$60/night

The Paradise Inn Windsor Palace Hotel is a great option for budget-conscious travelers looking for a bit of luxury. The hotel features comfortable rooms with private bathrooms, as well as a rooftop pool and spa. The Paradise Inn Windsor Palace Hotel is located in the heart of Alexandria, within walking distance of many popular tourist attractions.

Luxor - Gaddis Hotel

Price: $12-$25/night

The Gaddis Hotel is a budget-friendly option in the heart of Luxor's historic district. The hotel features comfortable rooms with private bathrooms, as well as a rooftop terrace with views of the Nile River. The Gaddis Hotel is within walking distance of many popular tourist attractions, including the Luxor Temple and the Karnak Temple Complex.

Luxor - St. Joseph Hotel

Price: $20-$35/night

The St. Joseph Hotel is a budget-friendly option in the heart of Luxor. The hotel features comfortable rooms with private bathrooms, as well as a rooftop terrace with views of the Nile River. The St. Joseph Hotel is within walking distance of many popular tourist attractions, including the Luxor Museum and the Colossi of Memnon.

Luxor - Bob Marley Peace Hotel Luxor

Price: $20-$30/night

The Bob Marley Peace Hotel Luxor is a unique budget-friendly option for travelers looking for a different kind of accommodation. The hotel is inspired by the music and philosophy of Bob Marley, and features comfortable rooms with colorful, Bob Marley-themed decor. The hotel also offers a rooftop terrace with views of the Nile River, as well as live music performances in the evenings.

Aswan - Pyramisa Isis Island Resort & Spa

Price: $50-$70/night

The Pyramisa Isis Island Resort & Spa is a budget-friendly option for travelers looking for a luxurious stay in Aswan. The hotel features comfortable rooms with private bathrooms, as well as a private island location with stunning views of the Nile River. The Pyramisa Isis Island Resort & Spa also offers a variety of amenities, including a spa, outdoor pool, and tennis courts.

Aswan - Nubian Oasis Hotel

Price: $15-$25/night

The Nubian Oasis Hotel is a budget-friendly option in the heart of Aswan's Nubian district. The hotel features comfortable rooms with private bathrooms, as well as a rooftop terrace with views of the Nile River. The Nubian Oasis Hotel is within walking distance of many popular tourist attractions, including the Nubian Museum and the Aswan Botanical Garden.

Aswan - Philae Hotel Aswan

Price: $20-$30/night

The Philae Hotel Aswan is a budget-friendly option in the heart of Aswan. The hotel features comfortable rooms with private bathrooms, as well as a rooftop terrace with views of the Nile River. The Philae Hotel Aswan is within walking distance of many popular tourist attractions, including the Aswan Souq and the Philae Temple.

Aswan - Keylany Hotel

Price: $20-$35/night

The Keylany Hotel is a budget-friendly option in the heart of Aswan's historic district. The hotel features comfortable rooms with private bathrooms, as well as a rooftop terrace with views of the Nile River. The Keylany Hotel is within walking distance of many popular tourist attractions, including the Nubian Village and the Tombs of the Nobles.

All of these hotels offer comfortable accommodations at affordable prices, and are conveniently located near popular tourist attractions. To get to these hotels, visitors can take a taxi or shuttle from the nearest airport or train station. Many of the hotels also offer airport shuttle services for an additional fee.

These hotels provide a range of advantages for guests in addition to their reasonable rates and handy locations. Numerous hotels provide on-site restaurants and cafes serving delectable Egyptian cuisine, as well as rooftop terraces with breathtaking views of the city and the Nile River. A few of the hotels also include extras like spas, swimming pools, and live musical events.

Affordable Guesthouses in Egypt

Egypt is a country full of history, culture, and unique landscapes that attract millions of tourists every year. The four major cities of Egypt - Cairo, Alexandria, Luxor, and Aswan - are must-visit destinations for anyone interested in exploring the country's past and present. To make your visit to Egypt more affordable, we've put together a list of guest houses that offer comfortable and affordable accommodation for tourists.

Cairo: Meramees Hostel (starting at $18/night)
Located in downtown Cairo, Meramees Hostel offers simple but comfortable rooms with air conditioning and free Wi-Fi. The hostel is just a short walk away from many of Cairo's main attractions, including the Egyptian Museum, Tahrir Square, and the Nile River.

Cairo: Cairo Paradise Hostel (starting at $20/night)

This hostel is located in the heart of Cairo's bustling downtown area and is within walking distance of many of the city's most popular attractions. The hostel features private rooms and dorms with shared bathrooms, as well as a rooftop terrace with views of the city.

Cairo: Pyramids Loft Homestay (starting at $25/night)
If you're looking for a unique accommodation experience, consider staying at Pyramids Loft Homestay. This guesthouse is located in Giza, just a short walk from the Pyramids of Giza and the Sphinx. The rooms are simple but comfortable, and the guesthouse has a rooftop terrace with amazing views of the pyramids.

Cairo: Sun Hotel (starting at $27/night)
Located in the lively district of Downtown Cairo, Sun Hotel is a great choice for budget-conscious travelers. The hotel features comfortable rooms with air conditioning and private bathrooms, as well as a rooftop terrace with views of the city.

Alexandria: Alexander The Great Hotel (starting at $30/night)
This hotel is located in the heart of Alexandria, just a short walk from the Corniche and the city's main attractions. The hotel features comfortable rooms with air conditioning and private bathrooms, as well as a rooftop terrace with views of the Mediterranean Sea.

Alexandria: Kaoud Sporting Hotel (starting at $35/night)
If you're looking for a more upscale guesthouse experience in Alexandria, consider Kaoud Sporting Hotel. The hotel is located in the Montaza district, just a short walk from the Montaza Palace and Gardens. The rooms are spacious and feature private balconies with views of the sea or the city.

Luxor: Queens Valley Hotel (starting at $20/night)
Located on Luxor's West Bank, Queens Valley Hotel is a great choice for those looking to

explore the Valley of the Kings and other ancient sites. The hotel features comfortable rooms with air conditioning and private bathrooms, as well as a rooftop terrace with views of the Nile River.

Luxor: Bob Marley House Hostel (starting at $22/night)
For a unique and affordable accommodation experience in Luxor, check out Bob Marley House Hostel. The hostel is located in the heart of Luxor and features colorful rooms and dorms with shared bathrooms. The hostel also has a rooftop terrace with views of the Nile River and the city.

Luxor: Nubian Oasis Hotel (starting at $25/night)
Located on Luxor's East Bank, Nubian Oasis Hotel is a great choice for those looking for a quiet and relaxing stay. The hotel features comfortable rooms with air conditioning and private bathrooms, as well as a rooftop terrace with views of the Nile River and the Luxor Temple.

Aswan: Iberotel Aswan (starting at $45/night)
This hotel is located on Aswan's Corniche, just a short walk from the city center and many of the city's main attractions. The hotel features comfortable rooms with air conditioning and private balconies with views of the Nile River. The hotel also has a swimming pool, a fitness center, and a spa.

Aswan: Keylany Hotel (starting at $20/night)
Located in the heart of Aswan's Old Town, Keylany Hotel is a great choice for those looking for a more traditional and authentic experience. The hotel features comfortable rooms with air conditioning and private bathrooms, as well as a rooftop terrace with views of the Nile River and the city.

Aswan: Nubian Island Hotel (starting at $25/night)
Located on Elephantine Island in the middle of the Nile River, Nubian Island Hotel is a unique and peaceful retreat from the hustle and bustle of

Aswan. The hotel features comfortable rooms with air conditioning and private bathrooms, as well as a swimming pool, a restaurant, and a rooftop terrace with stunning views of the Nile River.

To get to these guesthouses, you can fly into the main airports in each city: Cairo International Airport for Cairo, Borg El Arab Airport for Alexandria, Luxor International Airport for Luxor, and Aswan International Airport for Aswan. From there, you can take a taxi or public transportation to your chosen guesthouse.

Staying in these affordable guesthouses not only helps you save money but also provides you with unique and authentic experiences. You can interact with locals and learn more about their culture and way of life. Many of these guesthouses also offer excursions and tours to the main attractions in each city, allowing you to explore and learn more about Egypt's history and culture.

Whether you're a budget-conscious traveler or simply looking for a more authentic and unique experience, these affordable guesthouses in Egypt's major cities offer comfortable and affordable accommodation options. From the bustling streets of Cairo to the peaceful banks of the Nile in Aswan, there's something for everyone to enjoy in Egypt.

Affordable Airbnbs in Egypt

Egypt is a popular tourist destination with four major cities that attract visitors from all over the world: Cairo, Alexandria, Luxor, and Aswan. While there are plenty of luxury accommodations available in these cities, not everyone can afford them. Luckily, there are also many affordable Airbnbs available in each of these cities.

Cairo - Cozy Studio in Zamalek

This cozy studio apartment is located in the trendy neighborhood of Zamalek, which is known for its restaurants, cafes, and nightlife. It's just a short walk from the Nile River and the Cairo Opera House. The apartment is fully equipped with everything you need for a comfortable stay, including air conditioning and Wi-Fi. Price: $25 per night.

Cairo - Spacious Apartment in Heliopolis

This spacious apartment is located in the upscale neighborhood of Heliopolis, which is known for its beautiful tree-lined streets and Art Deco architecture. It's just a short drive from the airport and a 20-minute drive from downtown Cairo. The apartment can accommodate up to six guests and is fully equipped with all the amenities you need. Price: $50 per night.

Cairo - Colorful Apartment in Garden City

This colorful apartment is located in the historic neighborhood of Garden City, which is known for its beautiful colonial-era architecture. It's just a short walk from the Nile River and downtown Cairo. The apartment is fully equipped with everything you need for a comfortable stay, including air conditioning and Wi-Fi. Price: $35 per night.

Alexandria - Charming Studio in Sidi Gaber

This charming studio apartment is located in the neighborhood of Sidi Gaber, which is known for its bustling markets and street food. It's just a short walk from the train station and the Mediterranean Sea. The apartment is fully equipped with everything you need for a comfortable stay, including air conditioning and Wi-Fi. Price: $20 per night.

Alexandria - Bright Apartment in Smouha

This bright and spacious apartment is located in the neighborhood of Smouha, which is known for its shopping malls and cinemas. It's just a short drive from the historic center of Alexandria and the Mediterranean Sea. The apartment can accommodate up to four guests and is fully equipped with all the amenities you need. Price: $40 per night.

Alexandria - Cozy Apartment in Raml Station

This cozy apartment is located in the neighborhood of Raml Station, which is known for its historic buildings and landmarks. It's just a short walk from the train station and the Mediterranean Sea. The apartment is fully equipped with everything you need for a comfortable stay, including air conditioning and Wi-Fi. Price: $30 per night.

Luxor - Traditional House in Luxor West Bank

This traditional house is located on the west bank of the Nile River, just a short ferry ride from the historic center of Luxor. It's surrounded by lush gardens and offers stunning views of the river and the valley of the kings. The house can accommodate up to six guests and is fully equipped with all the amenities you need. Price: $50 per night.

Luxor - Cozy Apartment in Luxor East Bank

This cozy apartment is located on the east bank of the Nile River, just a short drive from the historic center of Luxor. It's surrounded by shops, restaurants, and cafes. The apartment can accommodate up to four guests and is fully equipped with all the amenities you need. Price: $30 per night.

Luxor - Charming Studio in Karnak

This charming studio is located in the Karnak neighborhood of Luxor, which is known for its ancient temples and ruins. It's just a short walk from the Karnak temple complex and the Nile River. The studio is fully equipped with everything you need for a comfortable stay, including air conditioning and Wi-Fi. Price: $25 per night.

Aswan - Riverfront Apartment in Elephantine Island

This riverfront apartment is located on Elephantine Island in Aswan, which is known for its Nubian culture and history. It offers stunning views of the Nile River and the surrounding landscape. The apartment can accommodate up to four guests and is fully equipped with all the amenities you need. Price: $40 per night.

Aswan - Cozy Studio in Aswan City

This cozy studio is located in the heart of Aswan City, just a short walk from the riverfront and the local markets. It's surrounded by cafes and restaurants, and it's the perfect place to experience the local culture. The studio is fully equipped with everything you need for a comfortable stay, including air conditioning and Wi-Fi. Price: $20 per night.

Aswan - Traditional Nubian House in Gharb Seheil

This traditional Nubian house is located in the Gharb Seheil neighborhood of Aswan, which is known for its Nubian culture and traditions. It offers a unique opportunity to experience the local way of life and architecture. The house can accommodate up to four guests and is fully equipped with all the amenities you need. Price: $35 per night.

To get to these destinations, you can either take a taxi, bus or train depending on your location. For example, if you are in Cairo, you can take a train or a bus to Alexandria, which is about 3 hours away. If you are in Luxor, you can take a taxi or a bus to Aswan, which is about 3 hours away.

The benefits of staying in these affordable Airbnbs are numerous. First and foremost, they offer a more authentic experience of the local culture and lifestyle. They are also a more affordable alternative to the expensive hotels and resorts. Additionally, they are often located in more interesting and trendy neighborhoods, where you can find great restaurants, cafes, and shops. And finally, they offer a great opportunity to meet new people and make new friends from all over the world.

Chapter 5: Top Tourist Destinations in Egypt

The Pyramids of Giza

The Pyramids of Giza are one of the most impressive and awe-inspiring architectural wonders of the ancient world. Located on the outskirts of Cairo, Egypt, these magnificent structures have stood the test of time and continue to captivate visitors from all around the world with their grandeur and mystique.

Built over 4,500 years ago during the Old Kingdom period of Ancient Egypt, the Pyramids of Giza were constructed as royal tombs for the pharaohs Khufu, Khafre, and Menkaure. The largest and most famous of the three, the Great Pyramid of Khufu, was originally 147 meters high and took an estimated 20 years to build using around 2.3 million stone blocks, each weighing an average of 2.5 tons.

The precision and accuracy of the pyramid's construction are still admired today, as it was built with such precision that each block fits together like a jigsaw puzzle, without the use of mortar. It's believed that the ancient Egyptians used a combination of advanced mathematics, engineering, and astronomical knowledge to design and build the pyramids.

Aside from their impressive size and engineering feats, the Pyramids of Giza are also steeped in history and mythology. The ancient Egyptians believed that the pharaohs were divine beings, and that they needed to be mummified and buried in grand tombs to ensure their safe passage into the afterlife.

Inside the Great Pyramid of Khufu, visitors can still see the remains of the pharaoh's burial chamber, complete with intricate hieroglyphics and artifacts that provide insight into the beliefs and practices of the ancient Egyptians. It's a testament to the power and grandeur of the pharaohs, who spared no expense in ensuring their eternal legacy.

Today, the Pyramids of Giza remain one of the most popular tourist destinations in Egypt, drawing millions of visitors each year who come to marvel at their ancient beauty and ponder the mysteries that still surround their construction. Whether you're interested in history, architecture, or mythology, the Pyramids of Giza are a must-see destination that will leave you in awe of the ingenuity and skill of the ancient Egyptians.

Moreover, the Pyramids of Giza are more than just ancient structures. They represent an important part of the cultural heritage of Egypt and the world. For centuries, these massive structures have served as a symbol of the Egyptian civilization and its contributions to human history. They have inspired countless artists, writers, and thinkers throughout the ages and have helped shape our understanding of the ancient world.

Despite their importance, the Pyramids of Giza are not without their challenges. In recent years, they have been subject to increasing threats from natural disasters, such as floods and earthquakes, as well as human activity, such as tourism and development. As such, preserving and protecting the pyramids is an ongoing challenge, one that requires careful planning and management to ensure their survival for future generations.

The Pyramids of Giza are a remarkable testament to the ingenuity and creativity of the ancient Egyptians. They are a must-see destination for anyone interested in history, architecture, or mythology, and represent an important part of the cultural heritage of Egypt and the world. As we continue to learn more about these magnificent structures, we can better appreciate the profound impact they have had on human history and our understanding of the ancient world.

The Sphinx

The Sphinx is one of the most iconic landmarks in Egypt and one of the most recognizable symbols of ancient Egyptian civilization. This colossal statue, with the body of a lion and the head of a human, stands on the Giza Plateau near the Great Pyramids of Giza, just outside of Cairo. The Sphinx is a truly remarkable feat of engineering, art, and religious symbolism, and it has fascinated people for thousands of years.

History and Origins

The Sphinx is believed to have been built during the reign of Pharaoh Khafre in the 26th century

BCE, although there is some debate among archaeologists and historians about its exact age. It is carved out of a single block of limestone, which was quarried from the nearby plateau, and it stands over 20 meters tall and 73 meters long. The Sphinx is thought to have been originally painted in bright colors, but the paint has long since worn away.

The head of the Sphinx is traditionally believed to represent Pharaoh Khafre, although there is no concrete evidence to support this claim. Some scholars have suggested that the head may have been re-carved at a later date, or that it was originally intended to represent a different pharaoh altogether.

Symbolism and Meaning

The Sphinx was originally known by the Egyptians as "Horus in the Horizon," and it was believed to symbolize the sun god, Ra. The lion's body was a symbol of strength and power, while the human head represented intelligence and wisdom. The Sphinx was also believed to have magical powers, and it was thought to protect the pharaohs and the people of Egypt from harm.

The Sphinx has also been associated with the god Thoth, who was the god of knowledge and wisdom. In some depictions, the Sphinx is shown wearing a headdress that is similar to that worn by Thoth. This association with Thoth suggests that the Sphinx may have been seen as a guardian of knowledge and wisdom, as well as a protector of the pharaohs and the people of Egypt.

Legend and Mystery

The Sphinx has inspired countless legends and stories over the years, and it has been the subject of many mysteries and controversies. One of the most enduring mysteries surrounding the Sphinx is its missing nose. Some historians believe that the nose was destroyed by Napoleon's troops during their occupation of Egypt in the late 18th century, while others believe that it was deliberately removed by the Egyptians themselves for religious reasons.

Another mystery surrounding the Sphinx is the question of what lies beneath it. There have been numerous excavations and studies over the years, but no one has yet discovered any hidden chambers or tunnels beneath the statue. Some people believe that there may be secret passageways or even treasure hidden beneath the Sphinx, but these theories remain unproven.

The Sphinx is one of the most iconic and enduring symbols of ancient Egyptian civilization, and it continues to fascinate and inspire people from all over the world. Whether you are interested in the history, the art, or the symbolism of the Sphinx, there is no denying the profound impact that this remarkable statue has had on human culture and imagination. If you ever have the opportunity to visit Egypt, a trip to see the Sphinx and the Great Pyramids of Giza is an experience that you will never forget.

The Egyptian Museum

The Egyptian Museum, also known as the Museum of Egyptian Antiquities, is one of the world's most significant museums dedicated to the art, history, and culture of ancient Egypt. Located in Cairo, the museum houses an enormous collection of artifacts dating back over 5000 years, from the prehistoric era to the Greco-Roman period. It is an impressive institution that attracts millions of visitors each year and is an essential destination for anyone interested in the history and culture of this fascinating civilization.

The museum was established in 1835 by the Egyptian government under the guidance of French archaeologist Auguste Mariette, and it has since grown to become one of the most extensive collections of Egyptian artifacts in the world. The museum's current location was inaugurated in 1902, and it was designed by the French architect Marcel Dourgnon. It is situated in Tahrir Square in central Cairo, a convenient location for visitors to access.

One of the most remarkable aspects of the Egyptian Museum is the sheer volume of artifacts that it contains. The collection includes over 120,000 objects, including statues, sculptures, sarcophagi, jewelry, papyri, and even mummies. The exhibits cover all aspects of ancient Egyptian life, from religion and politics to art and everyday objects. The museum's highlights include the treasures of Tutankhamun, the royal mummies, and the colossal statue of King Amenhotep III.

The Tutankhamun collection is one of the museum's most popular attractions. The tomb of the young pharaoh was discovered by British archaeologist Howard Carter in 1922, and it contained a vast array of treasures. Many of these are on display in the museum, including the iconic gold funerary mask, which is widely regarded as one of the most significant archaeological finds of the 20th century. Visitors can also see Tutankhamun's sarcophagus, his throne, and various other treasures, providing a fascinating insight into the life and death of one of ancient Egypt's most famous pharaohs.

The museum's royal mummies collection is also a must-see attraction. It contains the mummified remains of many pharaohs and their families, including Ramses II, Seti I, and Hatshepsut. The mummies are incredibly well-preserved, and visitors can see the intricate details of the embalming process and the elaborate funerary arrangements that accompanied them into the afterlife.

Another highlight of the museum is the colossal statue of King Amenhotep III, which stands at over 40 feet tall and weighs around 450 tons. The statue was discovered in 1928 in Luxor, and it is one of the largest ancient Egyptian statues ever found. It is a testament to the engineering skills of the ancient Egyptians, who were able to move such colossal objects across great distances using only manpower and basic tools.

In addition to these famous exhibits, the museum's galleries contain a wealth of other fascinating artifacts. Visitors can see the mummy of a sacred Apis bull, which was worshipped as a deity in ancient Egypt, or explore the galleries dedicated to the art and culture of the New Kingdom period. The museum's galleries are arranged chronologically, making it easy for visitors to follow the evolution of ancient Egyptian art and culture over time.

One of the challenges facing the Egyptian Museum is its aging facilities. The building has been in use for over a century, and it is showing signs of wear and tear. The museum is currently undergoing a major renovation project that will see the construction of a new Grand Egyptian Museum, scheduled to open in 2022. The new facility will be larger and more modern than the current museum, providing state-of-the-art facilities for the conservation and display of Egypt's rich cultural heritage.

The Egyptian government has launched several programs to protect and promote the nation's cultural heritage in addition to the new Grand Egyptian Museum. These include the opening of new cultural institutions like museums across the nation, the preservation of historic buildings and places, and the promotion of cultural tourism.

The importance of preserving and promoting Egypt's cultural heritage cannot be overstated. Ancient Egypt has left an indelible mark on human history, and its art, architecture, and culture continue to inspire and captivate people around the world. The Egyptian Museum is a vital institution that plays a crucial role in preserving this heritage, and the new Grand Egyptian Museum will further enhance its ability to do so.

The Egyptian Museum is an essential destination for anyone interested in the history and culture of ancient Egypt. Its vast collection of artifacts provides a fascinating insight into one of the world's oldest civilizations, and its famous exhibits, such as the treasures of Tutankhamun and the royal mummies, are among the most significant archaeological finds of all time. Although the current museum is showing signs of age, the new Grand Egyptian Museum promises to provide state-of-the-art facilities for the conservation and display of Egypt's rich cultural heritage.

Luxor and Karnak Temples

Egypt is a country steeped in history, and there is no better place to experience this history than at the temples of Luxor and Karnak. These temples are some of the most impressive and well-preserved ancient monuments in Egypt, and they offer visitors a glimpse into the past, allowing them to experience the grandeur and magnificence of ancient Egypt firsthand.

Located in the city of Luxor, the Luxor Temple is a massive complex that was built by Amenhotep III in the 14th century BC. The temple is dedicated to the god Amun-Ra, and it was a center of worship and pilgrimage for centuries. The temple is known for its stunning columns and carvings, which are some of the best-preserved examples of ancient Egyptian art. The temple was also the site of many important events, including the crowning of pharaohs and the celebration of festivals.

One of the most impressive features of the Luxor Temple is the Great Hypostyle Hall, which is a massive room with 134 columns that stand over 50 feet tall. The columns are decorated with intricate carvings and hieroglyphs, which depict scenes from ancient Egyptian mythology and history. The hall is a true masterpiece of ancient architecture, and it is one of the most iconic and recognizable features of the temple.

Another remarkable temple in Luxor is the Karnak Temple. This temple is even larger than the Luxor Temple and is considered one of the most important religious complexes in ancient Egypt. The Karnak Temple was built over a period of 2,000 years, from the Middle Kingdom to the Ptolemaic period, and it was the center of religious life in Egypt for much of that time.

The Karnak Temple is known for its massive columns, grand statues, and intricate hieroglyphs. The temple is dedicated to the god Amun, and it was a place of pilgrimage for people from all over Egypt. One of the most impressive features of the Karnak Temple is the Avenue of Sphinxes, which is a long path that leads from the temple's entrance to the main complex. The path is lined with statues of sphinxes, which are believed to have once had the heads of pharaohs.

The main complex of the Karnak Temple is a sprawling collection of temples, courtyards, and halls. The centerpiece of the complex is the Great Hypostyle Hall, which is even larger than the one in the Luxor Temple. The hall contains 134 massive columns, some of which stand over 70 feet tall. The columns are decorated with intricate carvings and hieroglyphs, and the hall is a truly awe-inspiring sight.

Overall, the temples of Luxor and Karnak are some of the most impressive and important monuments of ancient Egypt. They offer visitors a unique opportunity to experience the grandeur and magnificence of this ancient civilization, and they are a testament to the ingenuity and creativity of the ancient Egyptians. Whether you are a history buff, an architecture enthusiast, or simply someone who is interested in experiencing the wonders of the world, the temples of Luxor and Karnak are not to be missed.

The Temple of Philae

The Temple of Philae is an ancient Egyptian temple complex located on the island of Philae in the Nile River, just south of Aswan. It was built during the Ptolemaic dynasty, which ruled Egypt from 305 BC to 30 BC, and is one of the most impressive examples of Egyptian architecture in existence today.

The temple complex was dedicated to the goddess Isis, who was one of the most important deities in the ancient Egyptian pantheon. Isis was believed to be the wife of Osiris, the god of the afterlife, and the mother of Horus, the god of the sky. The Temple of Philae was built to honor her and to serve as a center of worship for her followers.

The temple complex is made up of several buildings, including the main temple, which is dedicated to Isis, as well as a smaller temple dedicated to Hathor, the goddess of love and joy. The main temple is an impressive structure with towering columns, intricate carvings, and colorful hieroglyphs covering the walls. The temple was built on a high platform to protect it from flooding, and visitors today can still see the marks on the walls from previous floods.

One of the most striking features of the Temple of Philae is the way it blends Egyptian and Greco-Roman styles. The Ptolemaic dynasty was Greek in origin, and they brought with them a different aesthetic than the previous Egyptian rulers. The result is a temple that has both the grandeur and scale of Egyptian architecture, as well as the intricate detail and delicate beauty of Greek and Roman styles.

The Temple of Philae was a center of worship for hundreds of years, but it eventually fell out of use as Christianity became the dominant religion in Egypt. By the 6th century AD, the temple had been abandoned and left to decay. Over the centuries, the temple was damaged by earthquakes, floods, and looting, and much of it was buried under sand and debris.

It wasn't until the 19th century that the Temple of Philae was rediscovered and restored. In the 1800s, the construction of the Aswan Dam threatened to flood the island of Philae, and the temple complex was at risk of being lost forever. A massive international effort was launched to save the temple, and in the 1960s, the temple was moved piece by piece to a nearby island that was higher and drier.

Today, the Temple of Philae is a UNESCO World Heritage Site and a popular destination for tourists visiting Egypt. Visitors can explore the temple complex and marvel at the beauty and craftsmanship of this ancient structure. They can also learn about the history of the temple and its significance in Egyptian religion and culture.

The Temple of Philae is significant not just for its historical and cultural significance, but also as a location for research on the impacts of climate change. The Temple of Philae and other ancient Egyptian structures have suffered damage as a result of the Aswan Dam's alteration to the Nile River's flow and rise in water levels. Scientists aim to learn more about how to save these priceless cultural artifacts for future generations by researching how climate change is affecting this temple and others like it.

The Temple of Philae is an outstanding illustration of ancient Egyptian innovation, originality, and artistic ability, to sum up. Anyone interested in the history and culture of India should pay it a visit because of its magnificent architecture, complex sculptures, and lengthy history. By preserving and studying this remarkable structure, we can learn more about the past and better understand the challenges we face in preserving our shared cultural heritage for the future.

The Red Sea Coast

The Red Sea Coast is a stunning destination located in the northern part of Africa, stretching from Egypt to Eritrea. This 1,200 km long coastline is renowned for its crystal clear waters, vibrant coral reefs, and a myriad of marine life. The region's warm climate, coupled with its natural beauty, has made it a popular tourist destination for decades.

The Red Sea Coast offers visitors an opportunity to explore its diverse range of attractions. From ancient ruins to modern resorts, there is something for everyone. For those who seek adventure, the region offers a wide range of water sports, including scuba diving, snorkeling, and windsurfing. The warm waters of the Red Sea are home to an array of exotic marine life, including tropical fish, dolphins, sharks, and turtles.

One of the most popular destinations along the Red Sea Coast is Egypt's Hurghada. This city is known for its luxurious resorts, pristine beaches, and world-class diving opportunities. The city is also home to the Giftun Islands, a protected marine park that boasts some of the most beautiful coral reefs in the world. Visitors can take a day trip to the islands to explore the underwater world, swim with dolphins, or simply soak up the sun.

Another popular destination along the Red Sea Coast is the city of Sharm El-Sheikh in Egypt. This city is known for its stunning beaches, lively nightlife, and luxurious resorts. Visitors can take a day trip to the nearby Ras Mohammed National Park, which is home to an array of marine life, including sharks, dolphins, and sea turtles. The park is also known for its stunning coral reefs, which are some of the most beautiful in the world.

For those who prefer a more cultural experience, the Red Sea Coast also offers a range of historical and archaeological sites. One of the most significant is the ancient city of Berenice, which was a major center for trade and commerce during the Roman period. Visitors can explore the ruins of the city and learn about its history.

Another must-visit destination along the Red Sea Coast is the city of Jeddah in Saudi Arabia. This city is known for its stunning architecture, including the Jeddah Tower, which is set to become the tallest building in the world when it is completed. Visitors can also explore the city's historic Al-Balad district, which is home to a range of traditional buildings and markets.

In addition to its natural and cultural attractions, the Red Sea Coast is also known for its delicious cuisine. Seafood is a staple of the region, with fresh fish and seafood dishes available at restaurants and markets throughout the area. Visitors can also try traditional dishes such as kofta, shawarma, and falafel.

The Red Sea Coast is a truly breathtaking destination that offers visitors an array of attractions and experiences. Whether you are looking for adventure, relaxation, or culture, this region has something for everyone. From its pristine beaches to its ancient ruins, the Red Sea Coast is a must-visit destination for anyone traveling to the Middle East.

Chapter 6: Outdoor Activities & Adventures in Egypt

Desert Safaris

Egypt is a land of ancient wonders and vibrant culture, where the desert landscape plays a vital role in shaping the country's history and identity. For outdoor enthusiasts seeking adventure in Egypt, desert safaris offer a unique opportunity to explore the country's vast and rugged terrain. From camel rides across sweeping sand dunes to off-road jeep tours through rocky valleys, desert safaris are an exciting way to experience Egypt's natural beauty and cultural heritage.

One of the most popular destinations for desert safaris in Egypt is the Sinai Peninsula, located in the northeastern part of the country. With its rugged mountains, dramatic canyons, and sweeping sand dunes, Sinai offers a wealth of opportunities for adventure and exploration. Travelers can choose from a variety of activities, including camel treks, jeep tours, and hiking excursions, all of which offer unique perspectives on this stunning landscape.

For those seeking an authentic Bedouin experience, a camel trek through the Sinai desert is an unforgettable adventure. Riding atop these gentle creatures, travelers can meander through sand dunes and rocky outcroppings, stopping at Bedouin settlements along the way to learn about traditional customs and way of life. These nomadic people have lived in the desert for centuries, and their knowledge of the landscape and survival skills are awe-inspiring.

For more adrenaline-fueled adventure, a jeep tour through the Sinai is the way to go. Skilled drivers take travelers on a thrilling ride through rugged terrain, including steep cliffs, narrow gorges, and rocky valleys. Along the way, visitors can stop at ancient sites such as St. Catherine's Monastery, a UNESCO World Heritage Site dating back to the 4th century, or explore the stunning natural beauty of places like Colored Canyon, a winding gorge with multicolored rock formations.

Beyond the Sinai, there are other desert destinations in Egypt that offer their own unique experiences. The Western Desert, located in the country's west, is home to stunning landscapes such as the White Desert, a surreal expanse of chalk-white rock formations that resemble something out of a sci-fi movie. Travelers can also visit the ancient city of Siwa, a remote oasis town that boasts hot springs, mud baths, and a rich history dating back to the time of Alexander the Great.

No matter where you choose to go on your desert safari in Egypt, one thing is certain: the experience will be unforgettable. Whether you're riding a camel across the dunes or racing through rocky valleys in a jeep, the beauty and majesty of Egypt's desert landscapes will leave you breathless. And with the chance to meet and learn from the Bedouin people, experience ancient history up close, and take in the natural wonders of this awe-inspiring land, a desert safari in Egypt is truly an adventure of a lifetime.

Scuba Diving and Snorkeling in the Red Sea

Egypt is a country steeped in history and culture, with a rich past that spans back thousands of years. But it's not just the pyramids and ancient ruins that draw visitors from all over the world – Egypt is also home to some of the most beautiful underwater landscapes on the planet. The Red Sea, in particular, is known for its crystal-clear waters, stunning coral reefs, and incredible marine life, making it an ideal destination for scuba diving and snorkeling enthusiasts.

Whether you're an experienced diver or just starting out, the Red Sea offers an abundance of underwater adventures that will leave you in awe.

Incredible Diversity of Marine Life

The Red Sea is home to a vast array of marine life, with over 1,200 species of fish and more than 1,000 species of invertebrates. The warm waters provide the perfect environment for these creatures to thrive, and divers and snorkelers can expect to see everything from brightly colored fish and sea turtles to majestic rays and even the occasional shark. The coral reefs are also a highlight, with an array of hard and soft corals creating a vibrant underwater landscape that's unlike anything else.

Crystal Clear Waters

The Red Sea is known for its crystal-clear waters, with visibility often reaching up to 30 meters or more. This means that divers and snorkelers can see the underwater world in all its glory, with vibrant colors and intricate details visible even at depths of 20 meters or more. The clear waters also make it easier to spot marine life, making for an even more immersive experience.

Ideal Diving Conditions

The Red Sea boasts some of the best diving conditions in the world, with warm waters and minimal currents providing the perfect environment for divers of all levels. The water temperature hovers around 27-28 degrees Celsius, which means that divers can comfortably explore the underwater world without the need for thick wetsuits. The calm conditions also make it easier for divers to control their buoyancy and navigate the underwater landscape.

Accessibility

The Red Sea is easily accessible from major Egyptian cities like Hurghada and Sharm El Sheikh, making it an ideal destination for travelers who want to combine a beach vacation with underwater adventures. There are plenty of diving centers and snorkeling tours available in both cities, with experienced guides and instructors on hand to ensure that you have a safe and enjoyable experience.

Cultural Experiences

Egypt is a country with a rich history and culture, and there are plenty of opportunities to combine underwater adventures with cultural experiences. For example, you can take a break from diving and snorkeling to explore ancient ruins like the temples of Luxor or the Valley of the Kings. Alternatively, you can visit traditional Egyptian villages and sample local cuisine, or even take a camel ride through the desert.

Scuba diving and snorkeling in the Red Sea is an incredible outdoor activity that should be on every traveler's bucket list. With its incredible diversity of marine life, crystal-clear waters, ideal diving conditions, accessibility, and cultural experiences, there's no shortage of reasons why the Red Sea should be your next adventure destination. Whether you're an experienced diver or just starting out, the Red Sea has something to offer everyone – so pack your bags and get ready to explore this underwater wonderland.

Camel Riding in the Desert

Camel riding in the desert is an experience unlike any other. It is a unique opportunity to immerse oneself in the ancient culture of the desert and experience the way of life of the nomadic people who have been traversing these vast landscapes for centuries. From the moment you mount a camel and embark on your journey, you are transported to a world that is both beautiful and awe-inspiring.

Camels are known as the "ships of the desert" due to their ability to traverse the harsh terrain and extreme temperatures of the desert with ease. These majestic animals have been used for transportation, trade, and as a source of food and milk for thousands of years. Riding a camel is a skill that has been passed down from generation to generation, and it requires an experienced guide to navigate the dunes and ensure the safety of both the rider and the animal.

The experience of riding a camel in the desert is one that will stay with you for a lifetime. As you mount the camel and it rises to its feet, you feel a sense of awe and wonder at the sheer size and strength of the animal. Once you are seated, the guide will lead the camel through the dunes, offering a unique perspective on the landscape that cannot be experienced any other way.

As you travel deeper into the desert, the vastness of the landscape becomes apparent. The sand dunes stretch as far as the eye can see, and the silence is only broken by the sound of the camel's footsteps. It is a surreal experience, as if you have been transported to another world. The heat of the sun and the dryness of the air only add to the intensity of the experience.

The pace of the journey is slow and steady, allowing you to fully appreciate the beauty of the desert and its inhabitants. You may spot wildlife such as gazelles, desert foxes, or even a herd of camels in the distance. The guide will point out the different plants and explain their uses in traditional medicine and cooking.

As the sun sets over the desert, the landscape takes on a magical quality. The sand dunes are bathed in shades of orange and gold, and the sky turns a deep shade of blue. The silence is broken only by the occasional call of a desert bird or the soft snorts of the camels. It is a moment that will stay with you forever.

In addition to the physical experience of riding a camel in the desert, there is also a deeper cultural significance. Camel riding has been an integral part of Bedouin culture for centuries, and the knowledge and skills required to ride and care for camels have been passed down from generation to generation. Riding a camel is a way of connecting with this rich cultural heritage and gaining a deeper understanding of the way of life of the nomadic people who call the desert home.

Camel riding in the desert is a truly unforgettable experience. It offers a unique perspective on the beauty and majesty of the desert landscape, while also providing a deeper insight into the culture and way of life of the people who have called these vast expanses home for thousands of years. Whether you are an adventure seeker, a cultural enthusiast, or simply someone who wants to escape the hustle and bustle of modern life, camel riding in the desert is an experience that should not be missed.

Hot Air Balloon rides

Hot air balloon rides are a must-do experience for anyone visiting Egypt. There are few things more magical than watching the sunrise over the vast expanse of desert, the Nile River, and the ancient monuments from the basket of a hot air balloon.

The most popular location for hot air balloon rides in Egypt is in the city of Luxor, located in Upper Egypt. The reason for this is simple – the city is home to some of the most incredible ancient Egyptian monuments in the world, including the Valley of the Kings, the Valley of the Queens, the Karnak Temple, and the Luxor Temple. The views from a hot air balloon in Luxor are simply breathtaking, as you soar over these incredible landmarks and see them from a completely different perspective.

The balloon ride usually begins early in the morning, before sunrise. Passengers are picked up from their hotels and driven to the launch site, where they are greeted by the friendly crew and the colorful balloons. The balloons are inflated using large fans and propane burners, and soon you'll find yourself slowly rising up into the sky, with the ground falling away below you.

As the balloon ascends, the views become more and more spectacular. You'll see the Nile River snaking its way through the desert, with feluccas and cruise ships gliding along its surface. You'll see the green fields and palm groves that line the riverbanks, and the distant mountains shimmering in the early morning light. And of course, you'll see the ancient monuments – the tombs and temples that have stood for thousands of years, still holding secrets and mysteries that we are only beginning to unravel.

The pilot of the balloon will be in constant communication with the ground crew, adjusting the altitude and direction of the balloon to take advantage of the wind and provide the best possible views. At times, you'll find yourself drifting just above the treetops, while at others you'll be soaring high above the landscape, able to see for miles in every direction.

The balloon ride usually lasts for around an hour, after which you'll slowly descend back down to the ground. The landing can be a bit bumpy, but the experienced crew will make sure that you're safe and sound. Once you've landed, you'll be treated to a celebratory breakfast, often served in a traditional Bedouin tent. Here, you can enjoy freshly-brewed coffee, hot tea, and a selection of delicious Egyptian pastries while you reminisce about your incredible experience.

A hot air balloon ride in Egypt is an unforgettable experience that should not be missed.

Whether you're a history buff, a nature lover, or simply someone who appreciates beautiful views, you're sure to find something to love about this amazing adventure. So why wait? Book your hot air balloon ride in Egypt today and start making memories that will last a lifetime.

Hiking and Trekking in the Mountains

Egypt may not be the first country that comes to mind when one thinks of hiking and trekking, but the country has a diverse range of mountain landscapes that are perfect for adventurers seeking a unique experience. The Egyptian mountains are not only steeped in history and culture, but they offer breathtaking views, challenging terrain, and a chance to explore some of the most remote and beautiful areas of the country.

One of the most famous mountain ranges in Egypt is the Sinai Peninsula, located in the northeast of the country. The Sinai Mountains are a stunning sight, with jagged peaks and deep valleys that provide a challenge to even the most experienced hikers. Mount Sinai, also known as Jebel Musa, is one of the most popular hikes in the region, offering visitors a chance to climb to the summit of the mountain and experience a spectacular sunrise over the desert landscape below.

Another mountain range that is popular among hikers and trekkers is the Red Sea Mountains, located along the eastern coast of Egypt. These mountains are home to a variety of unique flora and fauna, including the desert hare and the Nubian ibex. Visitors can explore the canyons and valleys of the Red Sea Mountains on foot, taking in the stunning views and immersing themselves in the natural beauty of the region.

The Western Desert, also known as the Libyan Desert, is another popular destination for hikers and trekkers. This vast expanse of sand and rock is home to some of the most remote and isolated communities in Egypt, and visitors can hike through the desert to visit these communities and experience their unique way of life. The Western Desert is also home to several ancient tombs and ruins, which offer a glimpse into the rich history and culture of the region.

For those seeking a more challenging trek, the White Desert is a must-visit destination. Located in the heart of the Western Desert, the White Desert is a stark and otherworldly landscape that is home to a series of towering white rock formations. Hikers can spend days exploring the desert, camping out under the stars and experiencing the raw beauty of this unique environment.

When planning a hiking or trekking trip in Egypt, it is important to take into account the weather and climate of the region. Summers in

Egypt can be extremely hot and dry, with temperatures often reaching over 100 degrees Fahrenheit. The best time to visit for hiking and trekking is during the cooler months of November through March, when temperatures are more moderate and comfortable.

It is also important to take the necessary precautions when hiking and trekking in Egypt, including bringing plenty of water and food, wearing appropriate clothing and footwear, and following any local regulations or guidelines. Hiring a local guide is also highly recommended, as they can provide valuable insights into the region and ensure a safe and enjoyable experience.

Hiking and trekking in the Egyptian mountains is a unique and unforgettable experience that offers a chance to explore some of the most remote and beautiful landscapes in the country. Whether you are a seasoned hiker or a first-time adventurer, the Egyptian mountains are sure to provide a challenge and a sense of wonder that will stay with you for years to come.

Chapter 7: Practical Information for Travelers

Language and Communication

As a tourist visiting Egypt, it is important to understand the country's language and communication to fully immerse yourself in the Egyptian experience. Here are some important things to know about language and communication in Egypt:

The Official Language

Arabic is the official language of Egypt, and it is the most commonly spoken language in the country. Egyptian Arabic, however, has its own unique dialect that may differ from the standard Arabic language that is spoken in other Arab countries. It is important to note that while many people in Egypt speak English, especially in tourist areas, it is always helpful to learn some basic Arabic phrases.

Common Arabic Phrases

Here are some useful Arabic phrases that you might need during your visit to Egypt:

Salam Alaikum: This is a common greeting in Arabic that means "peace be upon you." You can use this phrase to greet people you meet in Egypt.

Shukran: This is the Arabic word for "thank you." It is always polite to say shukran when someone does something for you.

Afwan: This is the Arabic word for "you're welcome." It is the appropriate response when someone says shukran to you.

Min Fadlak: This phrase means "please" and is often used when asking for something politely.

Laa Shukran: This phrase means "no, thank you" and can be used when you don't want something that is being offered to you.

Sabah Al-Khair: This is a greeting used in the morning that means "good morning."

Masa Al-Khair: This is a greeting used in the afternoon and evening that means "good evening."

Ana Asif: This phrase means "I'm sorry" and can be used when you make a mistake or accidentally offend someone.

Tourist-Friendly Language

English is widely spoken in tourist areas of Egypt, so it is possible to communicate with locals in English. However, not everyone speaks English, so it's always helpful to have some basic Arabic phrases handy. Additionally, it's worth noting that signs and menus in tourist areas are often written in English.

Language Barriers

Although many people in Egypt speak English, language barriers can still be an issue. It is not uncommon for misunderstandings to occur due to differences in dialects or pronunciation. In these situations, it is important to remain patient and polite. Sometimes, using gestures or pointing can help you communicate effectively.

Egyptian Gestures

Egyptians use many hand gestures to communicate, and some of these gestures may not be familiar to foreigners. For example, pointing with your index finger is considered impolite in Egypt, so it's best to use your whole hand instead. Additionally, it's common for Egyptians to touch their nose or chin when they are thinking, and to use a thumbs-up gesture to indicate agreement.

While Arabic is the official language of Egypt, English is widely spoken in tourist areas. However, it's always helpful to learn some basic Arabic phrases to communicate effectively and show respect for the local culture. When language barriers do occur, remain patient and polite, and don't hesitate to use gestures to help you communicate. By understanding the language and communication in Egypt, you can have a more enjoyable and fulfilling experience during your visit to this incredible country.

Etiquette and Customs

Egypt is a land of ancient history, bustling cities, and a rich culture that has been shaped by thousands of years of tradition. As a tourist visiting Egypt, it is important to understand the country's etiquette and customs in order to fully immerse yourself in the local culture and avoid any misunderstandings or offense.

Dress Code

Egypt is a predominantly Muslim country, and as such, it is important to be respectful of local customs when it comes to dress. In general, it is best to avoid wearing revealing clothing, especially when visiting religious sites. Women should cover their shoulders, wear long skirts or pants, and bring a scarf or shawl to cover their heads if needed. Men should also avoid shorts and sleeveless tops.

Greetings

In Egypt, greetings are an important part of social interaction. When meeting someone for the first time, it is customary to shake hands and say "as-salaam alaykum" which means "peace be upon you". If you are addressing an older person, it is polite to add "aunt" or "uncle" before their name.

Gift-giving

Gift-giving is a common practice in Egypt, and it is considered a sign of respect and hospitality. If you are invited to someone's home, it is customary to bring a small gift such as a box of chocolates or a bouquet of flowers. When presenting the gift, it is polite to use your right hand or both hands.

Food and Drink

Egyptian cuisine is delicious and diverse, but it is important to be aware of certain customs when dining out. When eating with your hands, it is considered polite to use your right hand only, as the left hand is considered unclean. It is also customary to remove your shoes before entering someone's home.

Respect for Religious Sites

Egypt is home to many important religious sites, including mosques and temples, and it is important to be respectful when visiting these places. When entering a mosque, it is customary to remove your shoes and dress conservatively. It is also important to be quiet and respectful of those who are praying.

Bargaining

Bargaining is a common practice in Egypt, and it is expected in many markets and shops. When bargaining, it is important to remain polite and respectful. Start by offering a price that is lower than the asking price, and negotiate from there. Remember that haggling is part of the culture, so don't take offense if the seller appears to be playing hardball.

Language

While many Egyptians speak English, it is always polite to learn a few basic phrases in Arabic. This shows that you are making an effort to engage with the local culture and will be appreciated by those you meet. Some common phrases include "shukran" (thank you), "marhaba" (hello), and "ma'a salaama" (goodbye).

Egypt is a fascinating and beautiful country that offers a wealth of cultural experiences. By being aware of the local etiquette and customs, you can fully immerse yourself in the local culture and avoid any misunderstandings or offense. Remember to be respectful, polite, and open-minded, and you are sure to have a wonderful time in this amazing country.

Useful Phrases in Arabic

Egypt is a fascinating country with a rich history and culture, attracting millions of tourists every year. Arabic is the official language of Egypt and while many people speak English, it's always helpful to know some useful Arabic phrases to make your trip smoother and more enjoyable. Here are some essential Arabic phrases you should know when visiting Egypt:

Greetings and Basic Phrases

It's always polite to start any conversation with a greeting. In Egypt, people usually greet each other by saying "As-salaam Alaikum," which means "Peace be upon you." The response to this greeting is "Wa alaikum as-salaam," which means "And peace be upon you too." Other basic phrases you might find useful include:

Shukran: Thank you
Afwan: You're welcome
Ahlan wa sahlan: Welcome

Ma'a salama: Goodbye
Sabah al-khayr: Good morning
Masa al-khayr: Good evening

Getting Around

If you plan to explore Egypt, you'll need to know some phrases to help you navigate the country. Here are some helpful phrases to get you started:

Fein…?: Where is…?
Al-metro lein?: Where is the metro?
Taxi!: Taxi!
Ana a'ayiz ashrab mai: I'd like to have some water.
Kam da'rak?: How much does it cost?
Yameen: Right
Shemaal: Left

Food and Drinks

Egyptian cuisine is delicious and diverse, so you're bound to come across some new and exciting dishes during your trip. Here are some Arabic phrases that will help you navigate menus and order food and drinks:

Al-'ashaa lana!: We're hungry!
Al-mata'am fein?: Where is the restaurant?
Menu, min faDlik: Menu, please.
Ana a'ayiz: I'd like...
Khamr: Wine
Bi'ra: Beer
Ma' zaytoun: Olive oil
Sah'tayn!: Bon appétit!

Shopping

If you're planning to do some shopping in Egypt, knowing some Arabic phrases will help you communicate with vendors and negotiate prices. Here are some phrases to get you started:

Ana ba'ayiz da: I want this.
Kam as-sa'ar?: What's the price?
Mumkin tesawerly safra ad-donia?: Can you give me a discount?
La shukran: No, thank you.
Shukran, ghalebtholy!: Thank you, you convinced me!

Emergency Situations

While Egypt is generally a safe country, it's always good to be prepared for emergencies. Here are some Arabic phrases that may come in handy:

Musa'ada!: Help!
Ta'assar: Emergency
Doktor!: Doctor!
Shurta!: Police!
Ana moo befadl: I'm not interested.
La afham: I don't understand.

Learning some Arabic phrases will not only help you communicate better with locals during your visit to Egypt but will also show that you respect their culture. Remember, Egyptians are friendly and welcoming people, and a little effort to speak their language can go a long way in building positive relationships.

Electricity and Plugs

If you're planning to visit Egypt, it's essential to know about the country's electricity and plugs to avoid any inconvenience during your trip. Here, we'll cover everything a tourist visiting Egypt should know about electricity and plugs.

Egypt's Electrical System

Egypt operates on a 220-volt electrical system, which means that the voltage in the country is different from what you might be used to in your home country. Most appliances designed for use in Egypt will work with this voltage, but if you're planning to bring your own devices, it's essential to check if they are compatible with 220 volts.

Plugs and Outlets in Egypt

The plugs and outlets used in Egypt are different from those used in most other countries. In

Egypt, the standard plug type is the Type C plug, which is a two-pin plug that is commonly used throughout Europe. However, you may also come across Type F and Type E plugs, which are also used in some parts of Europe.

If you're traveling from the United States, Canada, or any other country that uses a different type of plug, you'll need to bring an adapter to use your devices in Egypt. These adapters are widely available at electronics stores, airports, and online retailers, and they're relatively inexpensive.

Power Outages in Egypt

Power outages are not uncommon in Egypt, particularly during the summer months when the demand for electricity is high. These outages can last for several hours, so it's essential to be prepared for them. It's a good idea to carry a flashlight and extra batteries with you at all times, especially if you're planning to travel outside of major cities.

In addition, many hotels and other accommodations in Egypt have backup generators, so you may not be without electricity for too long if there is a power outage.

Safety Precautions:
As with any country, it's essential to take safety precautions when using electricity in Egypt. Here are a few tips to keep in mind:

Avoid using appliances with frayed cords or damaged plugs.

Always turn off appliances and unplug them when you're not using them.

Don't overload electrical outlets or use extension cords that are not designed for the amount of power you're using.

Never touch electrical outlets, switches, or appliances with wet hands or when standing in water.

If you're unsure about the safety of an electrical appliance or outlet, ask for help from a qualified electrician.

If you're planning to visit Egypt, it's essential to know about the country's electricity and plugs. Egypt operates on a 220-volt electrical system, and the standard plug type is the Type C plug. You'll need to bring an adapter if you're traveling from a country that uses a different type of plug.

Power outages are not uncommon in Egypt, particularly during the summer months, so it's a good idea to be prepared with a flashlight and extra batteries. Finally, always take safety precautions when using electricity in Egypt, and ask for help from a qualified electrician if you're unsure about the safety of an electrical appliance or outlet.

Internet Connection

Whether you are planning to visit the Pyramids of Giza, the Valley of the Kings, or any other famous Egyptian landmark, you may want to stay connected to the internet while you are there. Here, we will explore what a tourist visiting Egypt should know about internet connection.

First of all, it is important to note that Egypt has a well-developed internet infrastructure, with high-speed internet connections available in most urban areas. This means that you should be able to connect to the internet easily, whether you are staying in a hotel, using a public Wi-Fi hotspot, or purchasing a local SIM card.

If you are staying in a hotel, you may be able to connect to the internet using the hotel's Wi-Fi network. However, it is important to keep in mind that hotel Wi-Fi networks can be slow or unreliable at times, especially during peak hours.

In addition, some hotels may charge an extra fee for internet access, so be sure to check the terms and conditions of your accommodation before you arrive.

If you prefer to use public Wi-Fi hotspots, you will find that there are many free Wi-Fi hotspots available in Egypt's major cities, including Cairo, Alexandria, and Luxor. However, it is important to exercise caution when using public Wi-Fi networks, as they can be vulnerable to cyber attacks. Be sure to avoid using public Wi-Fi networks for sensitive activities, such as online banking or shopping, and always use a virtual private network (VPN) to encrypt your internet traffic.

If you need to stay connected to the internet while you are on the go, you may want to consider purchasing a local SIM card. There are several mobile network operators in Egypt, including Vodafone Egypt, Orange Egypt, and Etisalat Egypt, which offer a range of prepaid and postpaid mobile plans. You can purchase a local SIM card from one of these operators at most major airports or at mobile phone shops located throughout the country.

Before you purchase a local SIM card, be sure to check that your mobile phone is compatible with the local network frequencies. In addition, you may need to provide identification, such as your passport, to purchase a SIM card.

Once you have a local SIM card, you will be able to connect to the internet using your mobile phone's data plan. However, it is important to keep in mind that mobile data can be expensive in Egypt, especially if you are using a roaming data plan. Be sure to check the data rates and roaming charges with your mobile network operator before you arrive.

Internet connection in Egypt is widely available, and tourists should have no problem staying connected to the internet during their visit. Whether you choose to use a hotel's Wi-Fi network, a public Wi-Fi hotspot, or purchase a local SIM card, there are plenty of options available to suit your needs. However, it is important to exercise caution when using public Wi-Fi networks, and to check the data rates and roaming charges with your mobile network operator before you arrive.

Conclusion

Egypt is a country that has captured the imagination of people for thousands of years. From the incredible pyramids to the stunning temples and the bustling cities, Egypt has something to offer for everyone. A trip to Egypt is an adventure that will stay with you for a lifetime, and one that you will never forget.

The country has so much to see and do that it can be overwhelming for a first-time visitor. However, with careful planning, you can experience the best of what Egypt has to offer. The iconic pyramids of Giza are a must-see attraction and the ancient city of Luxor is home to some of the most impressive temples in the world. There is also the vibrant city of Cairo, where you can explore the bustling streets and markets.

Egypt is a land of contrasts, with a rich and diverse culture that has been shaped by its long and storied history. From the Pharaonic era to the Greek and Roman periods and the Islamic influence, Egypt has a fascinating past that is still evident in its architecture, art, and culture.

The food in Egypt is also something to experience. From traditional dishes like koshari, ful medames, and stuffed pigeon, to the fresh seafood and colorful fruits and vegetables, Egypt's cuisine is a reflection of its rich agricultural heritage.

One of the most unique experiences in Egypt is a Nile River cruise. This allows you to see the country from a completely different perspective and take in the stunning scenery along the way. There are also many opportunities for adventure, such as snorkeling in the Red Sea or exploring the desert by camel.

The people of Egypt are some of the most welcoming and hospitable in the world. They are proud of their country and eager to share their culture and traditions with visitors. From the moment you arrive, you will feel a warmth and hospitality that is hard to find elsewhere.

In conclusion, Egypt is a country that offers an unforgettable travel experience. From the ancient wonders to the vibrant culture and warm hospitality, Egypt is a destination that should be on every traveler's bucket list. With careful planning and an open mind, you can immerse yourself in the rich history and culture of this fascinating country and create memories that will last a lifetime.

Printed in Great Britain
by Amazon

24053176R00109